The Bruce
Alonzo Goff
Series in
Creative
Architecture

Process and

Expression

in

Architectural

Form

GUNNAR BIRKERTS

Process and Expression in Architectural Form

AFTERWORD BY

JAMES L. KUDRNA

UNIVERSITY OF OKLAHOMA PRESS
NORMAN AND LONDON

Publication of this volume is made possible, in part, through the generous
support of the Graham Foundation for Advanced Studies in the Fine Arts and
the University of Oklahoma Foundation.

LIBRARY OF CONGRESS CATALOGING-IN-PUBLICATION DATA

Birkerts, Gunnar.
   Process and expression in architectural form / Gunnar Birkerts ;
  afterword by James L. Kudrna.
      p. cm. — (The Bruce Alonzo Goff series in creative architecture ; v. 1)
  ISBN 0–8061–2642–6 hc   0–8061–2645–0 pb
  1. Birkerts, Gunnar—Themes, motives. 2. Architectural design.
  3. Gunnar Birkerts & Associates. 4. Organic architecture.
  5. Architectural practice, International. I. Title. II. Series.
  NA737.B53A4   1994
  720'.92—dc20   93–40030
                                          CIP

Designed by Carol Haralson

Volume 1 in THE BRUCE ALONZO GOFF SERIES IN CREATIVE ARCHITECTURE

The paper in this book meets the guidelines for permanence
and durability of the Committee on Production Guidelines
for Book Longevity of the Council on Library Resources, Inc. ∞

Published by the University of Oklahoma Press, Norman,
Publishing Division of the University. All rights reserved.
Manufactured in the U.S.A.

1 2 3 4 5 6 7 8 9 10

For Sylvia, my wife,
my daughter Andra,
my sons Erik and Sven Peter

Contents

P O R T F O L I O

Built Projects

Projects Demonstrating Design Process

P r e f a c e

WHEN I ARRIVED IN NORMAN on the campus of the University of Oklahoma, I was reminded of Ann Arbor and the University of Michigan, Champaign and the University of Illinois, and Guadalajara and the University of Mexico. I was invited to each of these places to lecture, conduct seminars, and engage in endless conversations. Looking back, I see that my views have been more or less constant over the many years of talking. Perhaps this has to do with my continuous primary involvement in the practice of architectural design and building.

My stay in Oklahoma presented an opportunity to collect and synthesize my thoughts for a series of lectures I delivered there. One of the subjects I talked about was my own creative process for arriving at the design concept, a process that mandates personal contact and heart-to-heart interaction with the user and the client as well as complete knowledge of all other requirements. I call this process "organic synthesis." In it, all the factors that influence the result are synthesized before conceptual combustion can take place.

The creative act is a very personal event and a lonely one, almost like birth or death. I like to talk about emotions and feelings, our intuitive powers, our ability to perceive and visualize, and our imagination. But, with all our powers, we still are vulnerable. We need strong support, a foundation that allows us to assimilate both the positive and negative impacts we continually receive. I like to remind the young mind that this foundation is formed from one's ethnic and genetic heritage and supplemented with acquired knowledge. We must thank our teachers for giving us the methodology, the information base, and the stimulation. In many cases they also become our role models. We can only create from what we are and from what we know. We have to develop self-confidence, and every accomplishment will bring us to a higher level of self-confidence. This in turn can unleash enormous creative ability.

I like to talk about architectural form, which can project a message or convey metaphor or symbolism. If it does, it is context-oriented, physically and emotionally. One of the starting points for generating architectural form is context. The word *context* refers to the physical surrounding or to a set of cultural ideas. One must be current and understand the Zeitgeist. I am, however, skeptical about meaningless experimentation with architectural history and equally skeptical about the development of buildings as status symbols. There has to be an evolution in architecture through the richness of historical conventions and typologies that correspond to the contemporary context. Architects are not omnipotent creators, but rather interpreters of building circumstances; they respond to the demands of place, purpose, climate, and available building materials and building technology. Allegiance to history and culture, and not simply the mode of today, is essential to the lasting quality I strive for in my architecture.

I would like to thank the University of Oklahoma for awarding me the first Bruce Alonzo Goff Professorship of Creative Architecture. I would also like to thank W. H. Raymond Yeh for his encouragement, my good friend Robert Lawton Jones for his support, Kay Kaiser for initial guidance and editing of lecture material, and Professor James L. Kudrna for his assistance with this publication. Special gratitude goes to my assistant Susan Trager-Brozes for her dedication and loving attention to content and detail.

GUNNAR BIRKERTS

The Design Process

THE DESIGN PROCESS

Organic is not the form, it is the process

ORGANIC ARCHITECTURE

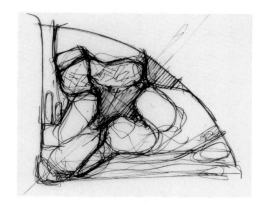

WHEN WE LOOK at the Modern Movement, we find organic architecture at its center. Surrounding the center are such facets as the international style, postmodernism, and the personal and idiosyncratic architecture of those who lost their practical bearings. Over the years, all these facets have been discredited in one way or another.

What is left is the organic core carried forward by Alvar Aalto, Eero Saarinen, Erich Mendelsohn, Hugo Haring, Ralph Erskine, Reima Pietila, and Hans Scharoun, among others. They were the romantic geniuses of the Modern Movement.

Until recently few architects knew about these organic individualists. They were out of the mainstream, and the architectural press didn't know what to do with them. These architects were idiosyncratic, but in appropriately expressionistic ways. Their idiosyncrasies allowed them to create freely and to make every building different. They stayed away from the major stylistic and philosophical

Concept development sketch for the Kemper Museum of Contemporary Art and Design, Kansas City Institute, 1991.

**Conceptual
sketch for the
Ferguson house
in Kalamazoo,
Michigan. It was
drawn while
flying over
Colorado on
October 29,
1980.**

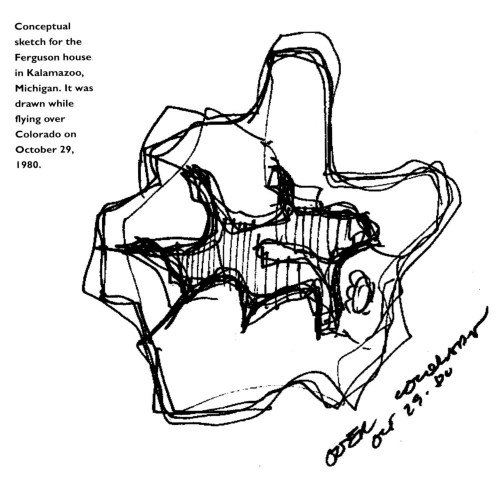

directions of modernism, an architectural movement that did not accommodate differences very easily.

Among today's architects, I would consider Richard Rogers and Norman Foster organic, although they happen to use high technology. So now you know how far I stand to the right or left, depending on where you stand.

I very much like what Fumihiko Maki is doing in Japan. In Italy, one must recognize the contribution of the late Giovanni Michelucci. In America, we had of course the very organic Frank Lloyd Wright.

We must remember that when the architects of the past did their greatest creative work, they did not have to fight the influence of theorists as much as we do today. They were themselves, and that's why we liked them.

A DESIGN THEORY will always tell you what to do, but I won't. I'm more interested in helping you develop your own process for finding solutions. Use someone else's theory and you get someone else's solution. Who wants that?

The most dangerous design theories are the narrow-minded ones that are based on some small aspect of design and do not take into account the larger base, the larger world, that you should be working with. You know the kind I mean—the ones that say you can do anything as long as you put the approved ornament on it. Some theorists make a religion out of one little aspect.

So, the biggest message I have for you is to stay yourself. Stay away from all the minds who are inventing architecture for you to do. You are the only inventor of your solutions—you are the overall synthesizer.

IT IS VERY DIFFICULT TO DEFINE organic architecture. It has been said that architecture is either organic, or it is arranged. Architecture that is arranged is only a building. Giorgio Vasari, the sixteenth-century painter, architect, and philosopher, believed that organic architecture was not built but born. The best modern definitions are collected in Bruno Zevi's *Towards an Organic Architecture*. Zevi quotes historian Walter Curt Behrendt's series of contrasting categories that define the organic and inorganic: The organic is the search for the particular; the inorganic is the search for the universal. Organic is anti-composition; inorganic seeks composition. The organic uses irregular forms; regular or classical forms are inorganic. Intuitive imagination produces organic architecture, and constructive imagination brings forth the inorganic.

The organic is the search for the particular; the inorganic is the search for the universal. Organic is anti-composition; inorganic seeks composition. The organic uses irregular forms; regular or classical forms are inorganic. Intuitive imagination produces organic architecture, and constructive imagination brings forth the inorganic.

I like to compare organic architecture to listening to a piece of music. You have to hear it unfold; you can't take it in all at once. If you tried, it would be just noise.

9/10/1991
SAS 711

Concept
development
sketch for the
Grasis House in
Vail, Colorado.
It was drawn
during an SAS
flight to
Stockholm on
September 10,
1991.

THE PROCESS OF ORGANIC SYNTHESIS

Real architecture has gone through a process of organic genera-
tion which I call organic synthesis. It is the creative force. It is
my philosophy and my methodology; the two are not far apart.

I used to say that I was creating organic architecture, but I real-
ized that I was misleading quite a few people. My forms do not necessarily emulate nature; my buildings do not look like mushrooms,
seashells, or snails. It is my method that is organic.

I use the process of organic synthesis to bring together all the
factors to be considered in the conceptualization of an appropriate
solution expressive of our times.

To simplify, let me say that there are certain forces working on the architectural form. There are inner pressures that give spatial or volumetric expression, and there are outside pressures such as the context of the region, the terrain, vegetation, climate, and orientation in terms of heat gain and light direction. Budget is a big factor along with the availability of various technologies. And to the list must be added the clients' needs and what they feel the building ought to express.

Pressures from within and from the outside determine a building's form.

A main ingredient in the process is recognition of the Zeitgeist, or spirit of the age. This factor is the most difficult to synthesize because of its constantly changing nature. It is also the factor that calls for the most moderation, assimilation, or adaptation by the architect.

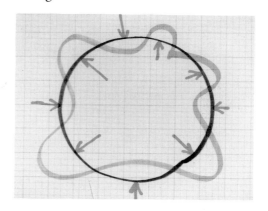

The architectural mind synthesizes all of these ingredients into a building concept. That is why the background of the synthesizer is so important. The architect's ethnic, educational, and genetic background always enter the organic synthesis.

Once you are totally aware of all the factors, it's as if you can draw a line

Once you are totally aware of all the factors, it's as if you can draw a line between the pressures that come from the inside and those that come from the outside. Suddenly a line forms that is doing something very interesting. It is the outline of the building form.

between the pressures that come from the inside and those that come from the outside. Suddenly a line forms that is doing something very interesting. It is the outline of the building form.

So that is how my organic architecture grows. Even our own physical and psychological development is based on organic growth principles. I believe that we are going from the past, through the present, into the future. We learn, develop, adapt, and create as we progress through life. Although there are many different definitions of organic, for me, the process is organic.

A specific language of organic architecture is spoken in Oklahoma — Kebyar. I speak another dialect of the same language, but because I am not a linguist, I cannot trace its formalistic roots. I can only tell you that the origins of my architectural dialect are in geometric form. We know that architecture is nothing but the square, circle, triangle, and line. In three dimensions, it is the cube, sphere, pyramid, and plane.

In my architecture, simple geometry expresses functional aspects of the project and free line expresses the particular, the unusual, the emotional aspects of the design. I work with orthogonality and linearity and then allow for the interaction of polygonality. It is always the interaction of straight geometry with the freeform that gives the project its expression.

Let me try to tell you about my design process. I don't know how other architects go about their design because we very seldom hear them give a full disclosure.

CREATIVITY

Creativity is that special ability to organize information in a way that enables you to arrive at endless variations on a theme. You take information and present it in unprecedented ways. If you don't, you are a plagiarist or an emulator.

Although creativity is tied to the architect's intelligence, it also is the result of his or her ability to collect information. The more you know, the more variations you can develop on your theme and the more creative you can be.

CREATIVITY ON A LOWER LEVEL is the conscious ordering, the shuffling and reshuffling, of information, images, shapes and forms, objects and thoughts. We go through the existing typology of the building we are working on. But on the highest level, our solutions are original. After we have gath-ered the information and have had some repose, we wait for the creativity to begin. Our subconscious leads us to the answer.

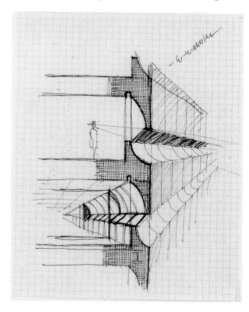

You don't know when it will come or what will trigger it. It can happen anywhere. It may be stimulated by an emotional experience, by music, or by something you see. But suddenly connections start coming like crazy. And you start creating because a catalyst somewhere started the process.

Given four building blocks, the noncreative person might use them for target practice, but the creative person would put them together to construct various forms.

I discovered quite late in life that the creative act is not a conscious one. Our conscious and subconscious minds only make contact with each other at short intervals — we call that

Sketch for the windows of the IBM office building in Southfield, Michigan. The drawing was sent to lighting engineers to calculate by computer the effectiveness of the reflecting plane. This quick sketch proved to be exactly correct.

thinking. But our minds work at very high speeds and sometimes without our knowledge. If thinking is not a purely conscious act, then neither is the creative process.

You can catch yourself being creative without being conscious that you are. One way is through color. Sometime, after you pick out your tie or your skirt for the day, ask yourself why you made that selection. Why the green one, or the brown one, or the red one? Color can indicate your mood, your attitude, or your disposition at the time. I believe that we are constantly developing color sense through education, through the practice of architecture, or through recognition of the messages about color and emotion that we inherited from our families.

We also use metaphor all day in very creative ways. In fact, we use more metaphoric language than straight description, as we are constantly comparing one thing to another. This is particularly true if you are an architect trying to describe what you have just done. You have to brace yourself against other people's metaphors about your work. You have to be prepared to hear people say that your building looks like an upside-down orange crate for example. Nobody ever says your work looks like a building.

The architect Philip Johnson asked me to lunch years ago and during our meal he gave me the business about my description of the metaphorical content of my work. He said he didn't know what a metaphor was. I explained that an example of a metaphor was me saying he looked like hell. That settled the question once and for all. We never had lunch again.

Symbolism is another tool. A symbol unifies many diverse elements in a simple and expressive form. If a building is meticulously organized and respectful of sound principles, it may become a symbol because it is so pure.

But you can't wake up in the morning and say, "I have to find a symbol or a metaphor today." They just come, if you are ready for them.

THE ART OF VISUALIZATION

I believe that imagination and the ability to visualize begin very early in life. When your mother read you a bedside story, you visualized the characters as she spoke the words. Her voice evoked images of all kinds—some pleasing and some scary. Children don't have that experience as much any more because television has taken the place of mother. We turn on cartoons for the kids and they have no need to visualize anything. It is all done by somebody else.

But architects also need another type of visualizing ability. I call it recall, or remembering. If someone tells you to visualize the American flag, you can do it. The image is in your memory bank. You can visualize pictures as complex as the faces of your mother, father, or brothers. As architects, we are always remembering and visualizing the square, triangle, circle, and line. When you get deeper into the process, you can perceive what the other side of the cube, pyramid, sphere, and plane will be like.

Any piece of design can be broken down into four components — the square, triangle, circle, and line — because these are the only elements architects have to work with. An analogy is music with its eight basic tones.

Any piece of design can be broken down into four components — the square, triangle, circle, and line — because these are the only elements architects have to work with. An analogy is music with its eight basic tones. Composers have written a million hours of music, thousands of symphonies, with only eight tones and they have never repeated themselves. Their imaginations enabled them to rearrange those basic notes. Architects find the variations with simple geometry.

To do this, we have to recognize the existence of the mind's eye, the place where the hologram of the concept is generated. We act out of what we see in the mind's eye. The hard part is expressing this vision verbally, or through the movement of the hand on paper.

IN THE LATE 1970S AND EARLY 1980S, I gave my students at the University of Michigan at Ann Arbor an exercise intended to deepen their ability to visualize and recall images from the past:

> I would like you to go back ten years in your life. Stand in front of the house where you lived at the time. You enter the house and you go to your room. Stand in front of the door, contemplate, open the door, and then tell us what you see. Where is the window and your bed? What kind of lamp is there and what is on the floor and walls? I want you to draw one or two perspective sketches of that room and the more detail you can get in, the better. Don't do this during someone else's lecture, but go home and really try to concentrate. It's all there in your memory; you can get to it.

I do this often except I'm going back forty-five years. I have very clear flashbacks of my childhood house in Riga, Latvia. I can recall every worn step in the stairs and the cracks in the walls where I used to hide things. It's very interesting how these memories come back.

An explanation of visualization and imagination involves daydreaming, an activity I believe has been underrated.

I told my students at the University of Michigan that daydreaming is a very important part of our lives. You are not a sissy if you daydream. We all daydream quite well about certain subjects. If you are in sports, I'm sure you have spent entire days playing basketball or swimming in your mind. When you play a game in your head you are always wonderfully able. The laps seem shorter and the basket is lower.

And when you are in love, you daydream all the time. It may make you worthless otherwise, but romance can enhance your ability to visualize. Dreaming about sex is no problem if you have a vivid imagination and heroic acts of all kinds are easy to visualize. You have probably beaten up some other guy in your mind on several occasions. If you can just start to visualize as clearly in your architecture, you will be right up there with the big ones.

We create when we dream at night, too. Unfortunately most people only remember their bad dreams. Learn to record the good dreams and to analyze them. Remember who said what and what everything looked like. These things are important because they are clues to the workings of your subconscious.

THE BRAIN

Now I am going into the deep end of the pool and you will have to trust me as I take you along. I have the feeling that not everyone realizes the full meaning of visualization. It is important to understand that psychology and philosophies are not exact sciences. There are no ultimate gurus in this area. We all speak for ourselves as we feel our way around.

To being with, the human brain is divided into two hemispheres—right and left. The left deals with sequential thinking, rational thought. It allows us to verbalize. The right side deals with intuition, space perception, and everything else we cannot easily put into words. In the beginning, long before we could talk, we worked more with the right side, the source of visualization and instinct. When we started writing, reading, and doing mathematics the left side began to develop and the right side to atrophy. In school, the pragmatic left side gets a workout, but the intuitive right side, the side that dreams for us and that would allow us to synthesize and use our creativity, seldom gets tapped.

We teach architecture by adding up the parts—one, two, three, four, five, six— then put a roof on it and it's a building. But there is more to it than that.

We are taught all about strategies and mechanical engineering, logistics, programming, computers, and climatology—all left-side endeavors. But on the right side, we are on our own. No one really talks about it, except in an indirect way. We could do exercises that might help the right side develop, but schools do not give right-side functions the prominence they deserve.

We teach architecture by adding up the parts—one, two, three, four, five, six— then put a roof on it and it's a building. But there is more to it than that. The creative part is something that we cannot really teach, but we can help students to become more aware of the potential sources.

If you operate totally on the left side of your brain, you will have a hard time becoming a complete architect. The same is true if you operate totally on the right side. Depending on which side predominates, you will become either a technician or a theoretician. However, ideally both sides must be highly developed.

You must sit in the middle, between right and left. From this vantage point you can take the information you receive from your intuitive, imaginative side and use it to bombard your pragmatic side. Soon the connections are made between things you have seen and memorized and the creative side of you.

When a person says "I imagine" or "I envision," he is actually describing a brain function. When you do these things, you're working with yourself, trying to bring something out from inside you. You have to be conscious that this is what is happening when you design. You aren't trying to connect with something that's on the outside or in a book but to find something that is within yourself.

Once you realize this, you will treat information in a different way. When you realize that what you see truly becomes a part of you, you will read much more eagerly, look through magazines more eagerly. And as you train yourself to retrieve the information, you will get richer every day. The best thing you own is your head. What is in there can buy you everything, if you use it.

In the early stages of an architect's career, the concept comes through sketching, endless sketching. You stay on it all night, compensating for a lack of original thought by evaluating your work after each drawing. You sketch something, the eye sees the drawing, and you make a judgment. Maybe you like it, or maybe you don't.

You make another sketch and another. When you can take one hundred sketches made on flimsy paper and stack them up and they all look the same, then you say *Ja,* maybe I have a concept. Sometimes there is a match between what is in your mind's eye and what is on the paper. But that is as far as you can go at the early stage of your development as an architect. The image in your mind's eye is equal only to the level of experience you have.

We all know the anguish of sitting before a piece of white paper and finding no force that makes you draw the first line. It is a mistake to just sit there. Please, draw at least two lines. Your hand is commanded by your brain and then the eye receives the messages and gives it back to the brain. The brain says it wants a third line. So you draw another line and another line and then you start getting somewhere. Soon you can start reading the results.

The biggest problem in your early student years occurs when you draw sketches of concepts and then try to blow them up to scale and

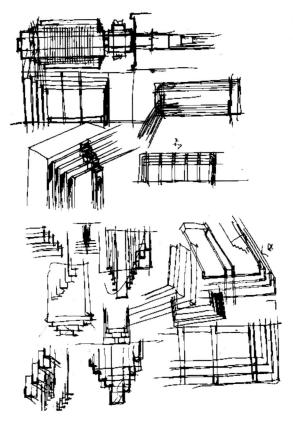

Sketches for the University Reformed Church, Ann Arbor, Michigan, 1963.

nothing works, right? That happens because your sketches are based on the ability to gauge scale and proportion that only two or three years of architectural education have produced. Once you have worked with these things over and over again, day and night for years, you will be able to draw your sketches and blow them up and be right on.

EXPERIENCE AND STARTING THE ENGINE

If you only know the letters A, B, and C, you can say ABC, ACB, BAC, BCA, CAB, CBA — all the variations of those three letters. When you finish your formal education, you know only part of the alphabet because you have had so little time to learn. Maybe you can draw from A to N, which gives you many combinations to work with. But later, when you know the entire alphabet, you can talk and draw forever. Just like a composer, infinitely rearranging the eight notes in music.

In my classes at the University of Michigan there are students who have never been out of Upper Michigan. Living in small towns, the most memorable buildings they experienced were their schools because they were in them for twelve years. They have seen glass block above a strip window, but that's about it. They only know a certain light fixture. The highest building they have seen is a twelve-story Holiday Inn, and for them it is a high-rise.

When I give these students a problem, what do they draw? They draw their schools. Their high-rise has the grid of the Holiday Inn. They have no more images. I accuse them of being image poor and tell them to get out and look around. We take field trips to Chicago and suddenly they know what a high-rise is. Of course I cannot tell them to go to Venice, but I tell them to go to the library.

Finding a full vocabulary works the other way, too. Imagine that a young architect has been living his entire life in Venice. Ask him to draw something and he might draw Doge's Palace, but this student would not know what the rest of the world was doing. As the Japanese say, the frog in the pond doesn't know the sight of the ocean.

You have to have the images. That's why travel becomes so important. The new images feed you and remove the prejudices that you didn't bring on yourself, but are there because of where you were born.

I did not have to read books to tell me about the history and evolution of modern architecture. I lived right within it. Riga, Latvia, my hometown, was one of the Hanseatic outposts constructed in the pure Gothic manner. From the thirteenth century on, it went through the evolution of architectural development on the continent and then it survived the Classical Revival period. Next it was influenced by the wave of National Romanticism from nearby Finland. The Bauhaus came, too, and that architecture was assimilated in an appropriate way.

The result of all this is that I have the history of architecture synthesized within my cultural heritage. It forms a beautiful base that allows me to work in a calm manner without making sudden discoveries of past styles. I do not go into convulsions after reading a book about a certain architect or direction that preceded my own. Because of this, I can draw upon past influences subconsciously during the creative act of conceptualization, but they are always synthesized through me. I am in control of the importance given to any factor.

I realize that I was lucky to have been born where and when I was. Not everyone has such a complete base to build upon. The best way to get it is to travel, but if you can't right now, there are other ways. I believe that creativity can be induced. I do it by bombarding myself with images. I go through magazines, through anything that has form and images in it. Architecture magazines aren't the only sources. A catalogue of Italian telephones and kitchen tools, or *Time* magazine can do it. If you look at a graphics magazine that's full of company logos, you will find every building plan anyone ever thought of.

I'm using the magazines as stimulants; my mind is not recording the images on the pages verbatim. I'm not looking at buildings; I'm looking at geometry. When I look at other architects' work, I'm not looking for what to do, but for what not to do. My greatest terror is that I will subconsciously extract something I have seen this way and it will appear in my building unchanged, without the benefit of resynthesis in my design process. We have to be very careful when we look at other people's images.

When you open a magazine, just look at the photographs and at plans and sections. You don't even have to understand them, or be conscious about it; your brain will put them together.

If I don't see the kids in the library doing this, I become very distressed. The library magazines in most universities look too clean to me. I don't think many fingers have leafed through them.

Certainly young architects tend to emulate what they find in the magazines. Emulation is unavoidable because they have not had the time to accumulate a base of knowledge of their own. That happened to me, too. In Stuttgart, my only contact with the outside world was through the magazines. I look at my student work now and it is full of Le Corbusier, Mies van der Rohe, and Oscar Niemeyer's Brasilia. There is a little Marcel Breuer and a little Frank Lloyd Wright in the details. I still have the copies I made of magazines showing glass pavilions built by architects in California right after World War II. The architects who stayed in Europe—Sven Markelius, Gunnar Asplund and Alvar Aalto—made my edges a little softer.

SELF-CONFIDENCE

Now I have to make a very important point. I believe that self-confidence, when it comes, unleashes an extra fifty percent of creativity. That's why it is so important to work within your own limits when you start in architecture. This will allow you to cultivate confidence.

If you know you can lift a certain weight, lift it. But don't put one hundred more pounds on the bar—you will crumble. When you jump over a river or a creek, if you don't have confidence you will fall into the water.

That is why I don't like to give complicated problems to my students. I don't believe that extremely complicated design problems develop their ability better than simple problems. I'd rather have them work on a simple problem, resolve it, gain the resulting self-confidence, then go on to the next problem. Giving students an airport or some other extremely complex assignment pushes them beyond their limits too soon. A sense of failure is the worst feeling you can have when you are doing creative work.

Also I am more interested in students' thinking than in their inking techniques. I'd rather give them many design problems and see them develop many plans up to a certain point than to have them devote weeks to inking presentation drawings for a single problem.

I have self-confidence in architecture, but there are other areas where I don't, and one of them is language. I don't worry about English because I can bluff my way through that, but I've been learning Italian and I've been having a hard time. I absolutely lack confidence in Italian, especially in the presence of someone who understands English and Italian. But when I am alone in Italy and no one around me understands English, I suddenly gain confidence and my vocabulary expands by a thousand words. In Italy I speak Italian quite fluently in my sleep. Yes, when I dream I speak beautiful Italian, I really do, because subconsciously I know all the words. I have heard them spoken for all the years I've been going to Italy and I have been quietly listening in.

One day when a street beggar asked me for money I just looked at him, thinking, Gee, I wish I could buy your tongue. Then I could have Italian.

I realize that the subconscious act of learning is involved in language as much as it is in architecture. There is a moment when you reach a certain saturation of experience of sound and vocabulary and suddenly you have the ability to put words together to form sentences. Maybe yesterday you couldn't say a sentence because you only knew the first word and the last word, but not the one in the middle. Today the word in the middle falls into place out of nowhere. But it was somewhere. It was sitting quietly in your subconscious until your conscious mind found a way to get at it.

GETTING READY FOR THE SWEEP OF THE LEAP

In the earlier stages of their careers, architects work analytically, including a lot of known good ingredients in a building. If you put in enough good ingredients, you end up with a good building. But at a certain point analysis gives way to intuition. The creative leap becomes more frequent with maturity because you have collected a base of information to draw upon.

For many years, I called that past experience my "baggage." Now I am told that the word has negative connotations in psychological circles—meaning that, for example, if you disliked your mother or father, that becomes part of the baggage you carry around with you. But I don't think of it that way. Baggage is your exposure to buildings, cultures, other art forms, politics, social science, and everything else.

Once that background is part of you, you can make an intuitive leap in design and it is totally justifiable. Of course, you always have to go back and retrace your steps because the leap goes over so many important factors. You have to backtrack and check off things on a conscious level.

The leap of the creative act is based on knowledge that you have gained without consciously recording it. I don't know if you would arrive at the same conclusion if you had recorded the information consciously and proceeded step by step.

At this point in my own career, after fifty years of absorbing information, I don't need much from magazines, or anything else, to start my engine. My subconscious mind directs me to the answer. But there are ways to induce creativity, or, to put it another way, to get to the information that you have stored.

The thinking process is going on continually, day and night. For me, it doesn't matter if I am awake or asleep. Just because I am sleeping doesn't mean that I'm not being creative, or not doing anything. No, my mind is working all the time. Sometimes I wake up in the night and I have the solution. I have to make sure that I don't forget it, so I write it down right then. If the solution is vivid enough, I get up and go to a place where I can draw.

This happens most often when there is pressure to find the solution—a deadline. When the pressure isn't on, then I'll get inspiration from music, or a glass of wine. Let's face it—wine allows you to put a screen between you and the other things in your life that are distractions.

After I have created, then I can turn on the TV and have a baseball game going on in the background and still I can work. But the creative process itself is very private. You are very much alone in it.

THERE IS A PROCESS FOR CREATIVITY and it's not a secret formula. Sometimes after I finish lecturing at a school, people say that the creative process I describe sounds too easy. But let's see how easy it is if they actually start practicing it.

There are three steps to the creative process: Research, incubation, and the creative moment. Research is the phase that I keep talking about all the time. You collect information until you can't stand it anymore. You collect general information from the events occurring around you in the Zeitgeist, but you also collect specific information about the building type you are working on, a library for instance, and about the site and program for the particular library you are trying to design.

There are three steps to the creative process: Research, incubation, and the creative moment.

You keep collecting and collecting, but a moment comes when you say that you have had enough. You are full to overflowing.

The concept is all-important. You cannot arrive at a building by adding blocks, one to the next, to the next, to the next. There is more to it than just the program, the structure, the mechanical systems, and on and on. First comes the concept, and then the other things fall into place.

Then comes the most wonderful phase of the process—the incubation. That's when you do nothing. You don't have to do anything because you have done your work. You listen to music to get the creative mechanism going, or you look at a dozen *Domus* magazines. If you're going to design a library, it's better to look at the issues with houses. That saves you from picking out images consciously. If you consciously select, you are probably going to select the wrong image.

But you really need the incubation time. This gets me into trouble in the academic community because in academics we don't give much time for repose. We give short deadlines and students must perform, just as they have to perform for the licensing examination board. But to do good architecture, you need the time to allow your mind to work before you start retrieving.

If all goes well, you arrive at the creative moment. The relevant material regarding the project is already inside you and now the subconscious takes over. You get a concept. And if you are ready, you make the connection between analytical information and intuitive solution.

The concept is all-important. You cannot arrive at a building by adding blocks, one to the next, to the next, to the next. There is more to it than just the program, the structure, the mechanical systems, and on and on. First comes the concept, and then the other things fall into place.

And who coordinates all this? The design mind—and, in most instances, the subconscious mind. In most cases we are dealing with an immense architectural and structural problem which we cannot possibly solve by consciously adding up all the parts. You could never, never, in your life possess enough knowledge to enable you to consciously attend to the 15,000 problems that are in a building. You cannot design the Empire State Building, or the World Trade Center by merely putting the parts or the pieces next to each other. No, first you get the concept, the goal, and then everything else falls in line.

And if you don't know about something, if your knowledge is zero, your logic will kick in and tell you that you need to ask somebody else about those things— acoustics, or elevators, for example.

I am only drawing you a rough diagram of the design process. At best, what I say is only a simplified version of the explanation. Remember, each problem that comes before you is your problem and you seek the solution.

USING YOUR OWN BACKGROUND

A strong factor in the design process is the background of the architect. Look at what happens in design competitions, for instance. A hundred or more architects may take part in a competition. They all work with the same program, site, and budget, yet every solution is different. The differences can be attributed to value judgments made by the conceivers, the creators. If you analyze the submissions, you will find that they express the enormous ethnic, genetic, and cultural differences among the competitors. We must be open to these influences.

The important thing is to be aware of yourself. Be aware of your powers. Be aware of your mind. We have all heard about people forced to leave their countries and everything they possessed and to start over again. They could do it because their most valuable possession was their mind. No one could take that away from them.

Be aware that you have enormous capacity to store information. We can make the comparison to a computer. You are carrying around this wonderful instrument in your head that is the greatest and most powerful possession you will ever have. You must treat it with great care because whatever you put in it stays there forever. It comes in through your senses and it gets stored. Eventually you develop ways to deal with this information. That is what we call the design method, or methodology.

The more you put in, the more you can get out. But what you put in does not always come out in the same form. It gets synthesized in the process. Each piece of information affects all the others.

If your father was an architect, for example, or a composer, it's likely that you inherited methodology from him—not his knowledge, but his methodology. So much depends not only on where you have lived, but on your ancestry.

My parents were in creative professions. My father was a writer and he was very interested in psychological subjects. Maybe that is why I talk so much about psychology. My mother was a linguist. I was exposed to their processes, their thinking processes. They were thinkers and teachers—that's what they did. In our house there was a lot of talking and storytelling.

I think we have to recognize the significance of genetics. We don't hear about it often, but when you look at the family lines of composers, how many Bachs were there? There was a father and all those sons and all of them were writing music like crazy. There must have been something in that family that produced the musicians. Some families perpetuate architects.

INFLUENCES FROM THE ZEITGEIST

One very important aspect of the conceptual process is the Zeitgeist, or spirit of our times. The Zeitgeist is the most difficult factor to handle in the design process because of its ever-changing qualities. It requires the most moderation, assimilation, and adaptation by the architect. This is why the background of the architect is so important.

I am in the middle of my times. I cannot escape it. It is in the air. All around me are the problems of society, the trends in architecture, war — you name it, it's there.

And I must react to it. I am reacting with who I am genetically and with what I have learned in my professional and personal life. All these things are working on you, too. You cannot be analytical about it. It just gets in you. And just as you are what you eat, you create from what you know.

I have two warnings, though. In organic synthesis, the value you assign to the information from the Zeitgeist is very important. You must discriminate during the process of acquiring information. At the same time, you must not exclude potential experience based on what you already know. For example, if you are Greek, Turkish, or Jordanian, you might be tempted to travel only to Greece, Turkey, or Jordan. Those places will have a strong emotional affect on you. But you should go to Finland, too, even if you don't fit in there very easily. Ideally you should go everywhere.

In my early architecture, I went back to my roots, to where I felt most at home, and that was Scandinavia. Then I gravitated down into Italy. But I haven't gone to the Orient. Maybe I'm not ready for that experience yet. So maybe I am discriminating. Maybe.

FOR ME, THE VERY DEFINITION OF ZEITGEIST is Vienna at the turn of the twentieth century. It was an expressive time. The architect Otto Wagner was working there. He and his compatriots knew how to live and they were not deprived in any way. The art, music, dancing, literature, architecture, even the food, all went together very nicely. That was their romantic Zeitgeist. I wish I had been there.

Maybe Charles Rennie Mackintosh and his group in Scotland shared the same Zeitgeist, but if they connected with the happenings in Vienna it was a big event. It was a long train ride from Glasgow to Vienna, and there were few magazines, no televisions, and not so many newspapers.

But now, everything is diffused and we live in a world that is less comprehensible, less contained than Vienna in 1900. We have a terrible time sorting out the information from the Zeitgeist. It comes in from all over. So how do we react? Either we close ourselves off and say, That's enough, or we say, OK, I'm going to let this thing in, but the rest is blowing my brain off. It's not easy today. Things come at you whether you like it or not.

I assign values to the information that comes at me, perhaps prejudicially. I don't want to know about the abortion issue, but I know I should know about it. I really don't want to know too much about the collapse of the credit unions, or the big wheeler-dealers who shape our lives on Wall Street. They are half-crooks, but I should know about them, along with the entire hypocrisy of the government. All of that comes at me on the television every night and it bothers me because it takes my good creative juices and burns them away. But you have to learn to deal with it.

I tell students that they always need to know more than they know. Students and practicing architects need to understand their own backgrounds and to educate themselves in the liberal arts and about other professions—even law and political science. Only then can we become interpreters of the times we live in and make value judgments about the information that comes to us. All those things affect what we're working on.

We must build a knowledge base for ourselves. We also need what I call the image bank. Why do you think that everyone comes back from Europe so elated? Because they have just seen three-dimensional images that represent hundreds of years of human history. People are affected forever by their first trips to Europe. The architects who created the buildings there were working through their Zeitgeists. If they were good, you can really get a sense of the times they lived in. If architects can't go to Europe while they are in school or soon after, they can see the images in books and in other publications. Of course you run into more contradictions in magazines.

Some say that the postmodernists are synthesizing the times, and maybe they are, but I don't think I like their synthesis. Postmodernism was just a reaction to the previous wave of high technology. The world became afraid of developing technology mostly because of the atomic bomb, moon explorations, and other space technology. Medical technology also scared everyone. Add together gene tampering, shooting for the moon, and the bomb, and the result was that everybody said, "Let's go back."

But they only went back to the imagery. Nothing was real. Still, that is over now. I think we can move forward again. The deconstructivist movement arose to push the postmodernists aside, and we are back to modern architecture again, I hope. A straight line back to the modern.

Maybe art is in the number one position for dealing with the testing of the frontiers of society. If you consider movies an art form, I think that just sitting through "Star Wars" and "Star Trek" puts you in a high-tech state of mind. You can't help it.

And if your kids are playing video games, they are growing up with this technology. What the result will be I don't know. I wonder about the effect of playing high-tech games in a Colonial-style house. Are the kids going to be confused?

CONTEXT

Before we can begin to understand the context of a building, we have to factor in both geographic and geologic influences. We have to know the orientation, topography, soil consistency, and vegetation of the building site. These are the first considerations. Then we can start shaping the concept, putting the building on or in, over or under the earth it must adapt to.

You must become familiar with both the country and the region of the building. You may know Scandinavia as a region, for example, but you also have to know the country you are working in. Denmark is different from Finland. You have to become aware of the country's culture, its historical background, its architecture, the availability of building products, and many other things.

You must go through an intense process of inquiry. A great number of factors ultimately affect the design. You have to find out about them before you start talking about programs, relationships, structural systems, and materials. But if you synthesize all the factors, they will generate the building's image, its face.

I have done this in Finland, Germany, Venezuela, and Italy. For the National Library in Riga, Latvia, the place where I was born and the one I know best in terms of its history and its ethnographic and literary past, the problem was that I knew almost too much. Everything couldn't be put in the same building.

Many buildings are designed without considering the context, however. When architecture is imported into a country by a name architect, or by a firm that works in a certain idiom or out of a certain dogma, contextual considerations may be disregarded.

Sometimes there are problems when an architect works in a foreign country. There may be signals that the architect cannot interpret. And sometimes the architect interprets more than the country is ready for. This happened to me on my first project in Torino, Italy. When I made a presentation to a large group of architects, educators, and developers, I went into an elaborate justification of what I had done. We really got into the vernacular with a meticulous analysis of the city—of the differences between the Roman grid and the military streets and of the forms of the existing architecture. I talked about the rhythms of the arcades and pointed out the unusually prominent downspouts everywhere.

After all that, an Italian architect stood up and said that it was odd that a foreign architect could be more contextual than an Italian. Then he said that maybe I was too contextual, that maybe the design was too resonant with literal images. That was possible. I explained that I took the arcades and broke them into low-tech stonework on the bottom and high-tech glass and metal as the building went up, but maybe the form language was too familiar to them. Maybe I was being too studied, too meticulous.

The client probably won't make a big deal about the fact that the building is in a particular country, or that the sun is rising on one side and going down on the other. Worrying about those things is the responsibility of the architect. In fact, most of the factors discussed here won't appear in the client's brief—unless the client is the United States Department of State, which requires that its architecture should express the United States and be congenial with existing buildings and culture. According to the State Department, architecture should not be overbearing. It should be compatible. They want to come in low, under the host country's radar.

In many instances, commissions for United States embassies come with a prescription to export American Federal architecture. But before I did that for the embassy in Caracas, Venezuela, I wanted to see what the local historical and contemporary architecture was like. The American ambassador actually wanted Colonial architecture, but after investigating, I learned that there was a problem in doing that. The Venezuelans didn't like Colonial architecture because they had been oppressed by the Spaniards. The indigenous architecture was primitive wood stick construction and buildings built over water. No one wanted me to do that, either. So the inspiration had to come from somewhere else.

After talking with Venezuelan architects, I learned that they considered themselves descendants of Le Corbusier, so to speak. They thought that the modern was their architecture.

My solution was to start looking for a concept in nature, in the stone formations of the mountains. The earth itself became a factor. The embassy was designed halfway in and halfway out of the earth with a face of stone that could have been carved into the mountainside. It was becoming a very indigenous kind of building.

Orientation was an interesting problem. When you talk with the Venezuelans about sunlight, they say they hate the sun. It is their enemy because it destroys everything. This was strange to me because I come from a place where you do everything you can to bring sunlight indoors. And the Americans in the embassy like sunlight. So what do you do? The problem was one of building orientation and sun control.

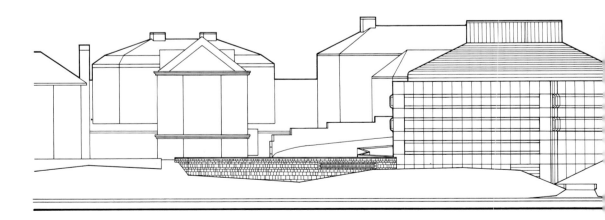

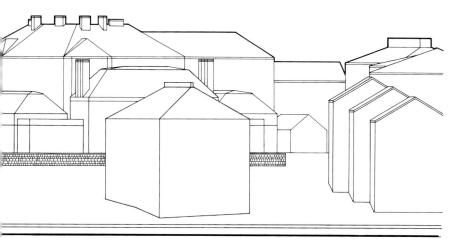

The United
States Embassy
in Helsinki,
FInland, 1975.
The drawing
above shows
the concept
metaphor; the
one at left
shows context.

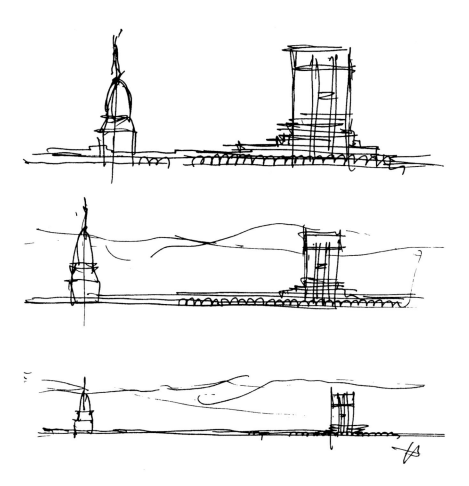

**Study of building
mass relationships,
Urban Center,
Torino, Italy, 1988.**

WHEN YOU GO TO A SITE, you try to see it from all possible vantage points. You find out about the traffic patterns by driving and seeing what you can see from the car. You examine the position of the sun. Which way is the east, the west, the north, the south? You look at the geology of the site and analyze test borings to learn if it's rock, sand, or muck.

Then you find out about the specifics of the site. Sometimes there are conflicts: the site is lower on one side and you want to put the entrance there, but then no one would see it from the parking lot. And sometimes you want to respond to the light in a certain way, but the site will not cooperate. At other times you want to turn the building to face the best view, but then the afternoon sun would roast everybody in the building. You can still do that, but you will have to control the sun using baffles, shades, louvers, or other techniques among many that are possible.

Next you find out that only half of the site is buildable. That there is only so much flat area and the parking has to go in one spot, whether you like it or not. Or there are easements going through the site that will push your building over to one side if your client doesn't want to pay a million dollars to build a road. Then, depending on the soils tests, you might find out that you have to build deeper foundations. The money to do that comes out of the total budget, which means you have less to spend on the rest of the building.

Slowly these pragmatic issues sink into your head. You can stand on the site and dream about it for awhile, but reality will interrupt you very quickly.

When I go to the site the first few times, I don't want anyone to distract me. I want to be there alone, so I can just think and really feel it. I don't want anyone else to tell me how wonderful the views are. I don't start taking photographs the minute I get there. When you photograph something, you don't really see it. You know that from your travels. When you see an exciting building you start shooting, but then you go away and realize that you really didn't see the building. It's the same with a

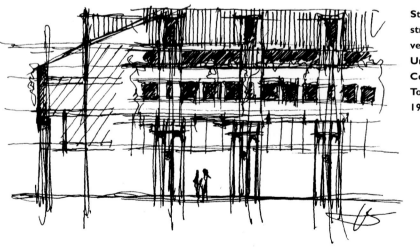

Study of street vernacular, Urban Center, Torino, Italy, 1988.

site. Only later do I take the camera out and shoot panoramic views. The pictures are for me and for the team that works with me back at the office. We splice them together and put them up on the wall. But often we will return to see it for ourselves.

I have to admit that when I stand on the site, I am getting the first notions of the concept, or at least a direction. This can happen if you have the experience to know what it means to have 100,000 square feet of building distributed over three floors, for example. And you are closer to the concept when you realize that you will have to stretch the building to get more daylight into more spaces.

On the other hand, I have done buildings that are in some ways in conflict with their contexts. In these buildings I have assigned importance to the edifice and to what it means in the city, rather than taking in every influence from the surroundings. In the evolutionary process of the city, surroundings may change. Older buildings may go; some may be gone in ten years. But what I have built will still be there. Because of that I have to make decisions that might suggest a building form somewhat out of the present context.

It's balance that one seeks. Responding or not responding to the context depends on what the building is, where it is, and the future of the area.

I HAVE BEEN ASKED about the contextual problems involved in grafting additions onto existing buildings by other architects. I avoid mimicking other architecture directly. In my opinion, that is not a creative activity and is a waste of time. We don't go after projects if it is implied that we have to build something's other half. But the problem, if addressed contextually, can be very interesting.

In 1964 I designed a master plan for the expansion of the Detroit Institute of Arts, a pseudo-Renaissance building designed by Paul Cret in 1927. The Cret building was a symmetrical, inflated type of Renaissance building that was very complete in itself. To avoid the architectural desecration of the Cret, I approached the building as a jewel in a setting. We planned to have the new north and south wings wrap around the back of the existing building. None of the new construction utilized any of the existing building walls. Connections between the old and new were made by bridges that penetrated existing window openings. The actual physical space closures between Cret and the wings were glassed in, taking the form of large atriums. The new floors opened like balconies onto the atriums.

My approach was to pay homage to Cret, not by emulating his form language

and materials, but by receding into the background. He had a white marble building while my addition was polished dark granite. Cret's marble was perpendicular to my granite, which became a reflective surface for the original building. Where the two intersected, each mirrored the other in a kind of double exposure. But Cret's general lines, the classic order of the base, shaft, and cornice, were maintained in modern terms and carried over to the addition, relating the new structure to the existing one.

Detroit Institute of Arts, South Wing, 1964.

I admit that I denied the tie to the Renaissance mother. The Cret had strong corners and I dissolved mine in glass. My roof is lifted off the wall by a glass strip for top lighting. That told people that the walls were not bearing walls, that the addition was a modern building.

So it carried two messages: I am modern, but I have reverence for the existing order.

Unfortunately, for financial reasons only half of the south wing was built, which resulted in a dead-ended, noncirculating space. When the north wing was built years later, my firm was not involved in the project, or in the decisions that gave the museum yet another noncirculating addition.

YEARS AGO, we did not talk about contextualism as a specific facet of design. Context was just a very understandable consideration that you worked with as you placed a building somewhere. You did not become a contextualist because you put the building in the right spot and designed it with the right proportions that recognized the character of a neighboring building.

These days, when architects talk about context many of them really are talking about ornamentation. But an ornament doesn't have to be a plaster molding just like the one next door; you can find ways of fastening stone or glass that creates a contemporary ornament. Modern architecture has ornaments, too, but they are made in a different way. There can be poetry in high technology.

As far as history is concerned, I think we have to leave something for other generations to judge us by. When the archaeologists dig us up after a thousand years and find entire postmodern cities, they will think we were pretty confused. It's like taxidermy, if you know what I mean. You shoot a nice animal, stuff it, and put it up on the wall. That animal had life and value in the past. Now that it's in the living room, what significance does it have?

THE PROCESS IN PRACTICE

My architecture does not have an overriding theory or style. Each project is conceived with its own sources of information and requirements. We are always starting from zero. I am the only non-zero, because at some point I'm going to make the decision to go one way or another. Someone always has to do that. Even if you are working as a team, somebody has to say the first word or call the play, or nobody would move.

Everyone in the office understands that we are starting from scratch almost all the time. Even if we aren't reinventing the wheel for each project, at least it's a wheel for a different carriage. Maybe that has become a unique characteristic because not many firms can afford to do it anymore. Most offices need to develop a continuity of style and typology of their own if the practice is to be profitable.

Our practice is not profitable. We blow everything. All the money we have goes into creating the next new thing. But that's where the excitement and fun is. That's exactly the reason why our firm has stayed alive and why everybody stays around. Nobody gets bored because we do not repeat ourselves.

Maybe we lose clients because they never know what they're going to get from us. I don't tell clients what their building is going to look like during the first interview because I don't know. When I say that, they wonder what kind of an architect I am, or whether I know what I'm doing. I try to explain that I can't give them a building description before I know what they need.

Everyone in the office understands that we are starting from scratch almost all the time. Even if we aren't reinventing the wheel for each project, at least it's a wheel for a different carriage.

But there are architects who will tell clients exactly what they are going to get in the first few minutes. Those who always work in their own style can say that they will do a white building like Villa Savoye and it will be just a little bigger and higher. But we can't do that. Every job is different.

In our office, we work in teams and the players change depending on what phase the project is in. The team designer and the project director, however, stay with me all the time. The project director takes on all the administrative tasks that deal with the client, consultants, cost consultants, and others who might be involved. The designer works with me. I generally bring in the concept after we have done the research together.

I am working on the concept from the moment I walk out of the client's interview room. I have already been told certain information that leads toward the concept. Then we analyze the program. For example, I know what 50,000 or 180,000 square feet would look like on a particular site. Put that together with the specific characteristics of the site and I begin to get an indication of where the concept might be going.

The building designer usually analyzes the program graphically, or with a model. At this point, the model has no form—it's just a rectangle or some other simple shape. Then we agree on what magnitudes to assign the information in the program. Frequently we go back and interview the client again if the definition of the need has not been clear. Then we do more research.

When I feel I'm full to the ears with the facts, I go away from everyone to conceptualize. I begin to look for signs of direction. By now, I am usually enjoying doing nothing while I wait for the signs to come. Sometimes the concept comes quickly, but sometimes weeks go by and nothing happens. But by now I know you can't force it out of yourself; you have to keep working at it gently and not be distracted by worrying about bills or a flat tire or what someone has just said to you. In the last few years I have come to realize the importance of relaxation and pauses in the design process.

Then a moment arrives when all the information comes together in a sweep. It is a very special time, almost a tender moment. I am talking about a completely sub-conscious phenomenon.

I can be anywhere when I find the concept. It doesn't have to happen at the draft-ing board. It can be during a meeting—I'm talking about something and I suddenly realize, Gosh, that's it! I honestly don't know what made me say what I did. And many times that one little phrase becomes the concept on which my entire office works for the next five years. And I said it in just a fraction of a second. But it was not just a frivolous string of words. It came from the deep subconscious.

That is the moment that I call the organic synthesis—when all the factors affect-ing the personality of the building come together in the right magnitudes and the building starts to grow like a plant.

The first drawing isn't necessarily pretty, but after you analyze it you see that everything the building needs is in it because it was created by your mind—which was full of everything you needed to know. Sometimes I call these drawings "blobs," but they are really the representation of my brainwaves. An architecture critic would call them seminal ideas.

Usually the drawing is not an image that shows a building three-dimensionally. It is just an image, a metaphor. Then we start working on it to get it into clearer terms, into a graphic form that begins to directly address the building or plan. Sometimes the concept isn't a plan, but is an idea for a section—something that stands for how a building will function, not for how it will look.

Then you go through a nurturing time in which you decipher your own ideas that are in the concept drawing. I am very possessive of the concept when it is first born, but I have to bring it out in the open and try to explain it first to my associates and then to the client. At first I stutter when I'm putting it into words, but as I explain, I am becoming wiser. I am beginning to realize what I have done. The con-cept evolves just like a little human grows.

I would like to make it clear that the subconscious experience I am describing applies only to finding the larger concepts that say what the building is about and give it expression. I'm not talking about the actual design of the building. After the conceptual stage I sweat over design just like everyone else when we are developing particular parts of the building. For that, it is the eye-brain-hand process, the same way we worked during the early stages of our careers. That's the agony part of architecture; finding the concept is the ecstasy. We have to have both, it seems.

CLIENTS AS PART OF THE PROCESS

The Residential Client

I have designed relatively few homes. The effort involved in designing a house is equal to that expended on larger buildings, but the fee is less. My office cannot afford to do residential work. But there is more to the explanation than money. I am only interested in designing houses when they present an opportunity to explore design problems that could be applied to larger-scale buildings.

Two of my first houses (Mequon, 1957, and Schwartz, 1960) were conscious attempts to break away from the frozen form language of Saarinen and Yamasaki. Many of my early residential commissions allowed me to experiment with geometries and lighting techniques that were later applied to larger buildings. I was finding ways to balance the glare reflecting off a lake on the west side of a house with skylights on the east side. The concept of different rooms "borrowing" light from the same window opening was explored in many of the early homes. A commission in 1979 for a house in Kalamazoo, Michigan, provided the opportunity to think through passive solar energy technology. Two months after accepting the residential commission, I began work on the University of Iowa College of Law, where similar methods were employed but on a larger scale.

Designing a house is one of the most difficult problems for an architect because it can become so private, so personal. The intimacy required between architect and residential client deters me more than any other factor. I am uncomfortable when I ask about the details of clients' lives. I also feel that I have to silence my own opinions because the house is not being built for me. To do an appropriate house for the clients and not stuff them into one that really is designed for you, you have to give up a lot of ego.

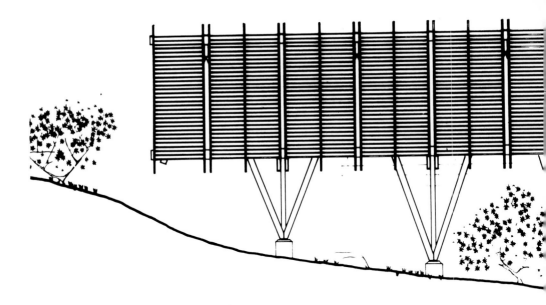

I seem to find communication about architecture more difficult with residential clients. Sometimes they do not say what they mean. Years ago a prospective client called and said she wanted a house just like the funeral home I built in Southfield, Michigan. The request perplexed and unnerved everyone in the office until they understood that she was admiring the pitched metal roof and the feeling of protection the funeral home provided.

Residential clients are usually a husband and wife. They do not always work as a team, as you can imagine. There are diverse opinions about the house, lifestyle, acquisitions, and expenditures.

The wife is usually the client representative and she has collected clippings of houses for years. Maybe the couple has visited Greece, Italy, and Mexico. Usually they haven't been to Finland, which puts me at a disadvantage. But they are very much in love with their pile of clippings and they want their house to look just like the pictures.

You have to be polite, so you look through the pictures. But I wish they would just talk to me instead. I am bothered by

FACING PAGE: Schwartz House, Northville, Michigan, 1960. The house was built to respond to the grid made by the four hundred apple trees in an orchard. The house was wood, but the image was one of concrete. The house was destroyed when the orchard was redeveloped.

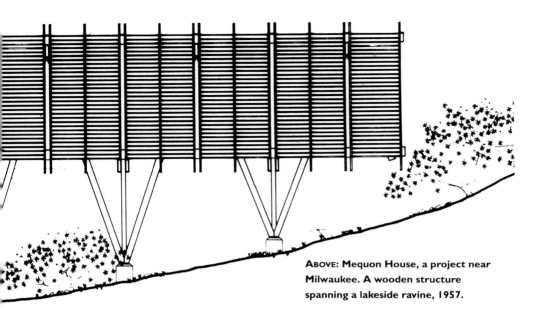

ABOVE: Mequon House, a project near Milwaukee. A wooden structure spanning a lakeside ravine, 1957.

images so early in the design process. I am impressionable and sometimes I can't shake those images.

What you really have to do is look at the pictures and try to figure out what the clients like about them. It isn't that they want Mexican tile or Italian tufa. Most of the time it really boils down to a few short sentences. They like warmth. They like to feel cozy. They want a good view to the outside, but they want to feel protected at the same time. Maybe they want white in the dining room and dark around the fireplace. Finally you get them to verbalize these things. Then you can toss away all those pictures and never see them again.

Sometimes when the two of them don't agree you almost become a marriage counselor. And the architect becomes a very important figure to the wife. She assumes that building a house is a role that her husband would fill if he had the skills. He would be the one building the nest. But you come in instead, and the wife tells you everything—where her panties are, or whether she wants to be in the marriage at all. It becomes very uncomfortably intimate. It's a difficult situation, but it has to be managed.

Thomas S. Monaghan and Domino's Farms

In terms of my synthesizing process, the headquarters for Domino's was the most difficult project of my life because I had to work with someone else's architecture.

I wanted to work with Tom Monaghan because he was interested in quality for the people around him. He wanted everything he had to be the world's best. He owned a car that won the Indianapolis 500 race. He bought the Detroit Tigers baseball team and it became world champion. And nobody delivered pizza faster or hotter than Domino's. He thought of everything that way, including architecture.

He believed that Frank Lloyd Wright was *numero uno* in the world of architects, and that was why he modeled his ambitions on him. But Frank Lloyd Wright was dead. That created a problem for Tom, and eventually for me.

He knew that I was an architect who carried no style from job to job. He thought I came to him almost as a blank. He could look up my past in books and he was not disturbed by what he saw. I can imagine Tom saying to himself, Yes, I can talk with this man. He's not pushing a standard line that he offers to every client.

But the bottom line was that he really wanted me to work in direct emulation of

John Merlin Williams

**Domino's Pizza, Inc.
Headquarters, Ann Arbor,
Michigan.** Aerial view of
early development above;
below, footprints and site
drawing.

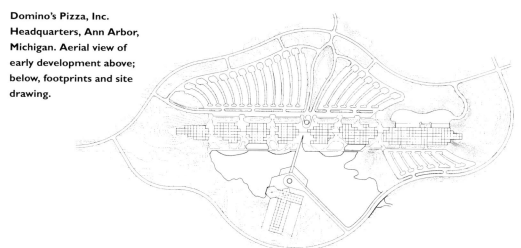

Frank Lloyd Wright did architecture so well that whenever you have a pitched roof with a five-foot overhang, you are halfway into his style.

Wright, and I couldn't subject myself to that. Instead, I took some of the principles of Wright and then departed from them—to bring them into the twenty-first century, so to speak, and to make the principles work for what Tom wanted to do.

I think that Monaghan knew I wasn't going to push my style on him. He also knew that I was not going to accept anyone else's style—Monaghan's or Wright's. He knew that I was open. But he wanted to see how far he could push Wright's style on me before I broke. That was his whole game. And it was a game.

I also think he knew that he would get something unique out of this mixture, this battle of wills. And I think he knew it was going to be an interesting wrestling match.

When we started together, Monaghan told me six things that he liked: Low-slung buildings, overhangs, brick, copper, wood, and berms. Direct references to Wright's prairie architecture.

"OK, give me those six things," I responded, "but don't mention Frank Lloyd Wright every five minutes and let's see what comes out. Just let me do it." That's how I told him I would approach the project.

After I signed the contract I stopped looking at everything of Wright's. I did not want to be influenced by something that did not come through my own process. I didn't want to be suddenly struck by some easy imagery picked up from a book. That's a danger that sometimes befalls architects, you know.

But I couldn't help it that Domino's is somewhat in the Wright imagery. Frank Lloyd Wright did architecture so well that whenever you have a pitched roof with a five-foot overhang, you are halfway into his style. You can't escape it. And when you have a long building that's brick, copper, and wood, what's left to do?

Monaghan's program was immense—one million square feet. The corporation was uncertain of its development and growth, so the building had to be flexible. It would have been difficult to fit that into an enlarged McCormick house, which was what Monaghan originally wanted me to do. Wright's Marin County Civic Center was the biggest built model we could look at, but that wouldn't work for Monaghan either. In order to deal with possible expansion of the program at a later date, a flexible system had to be developed. I drew from the idea of the railroad yard that allows you to arrange the cars on different tracks and eventually put a train together. The system's model we devised shows seven twenty-eight-foot-wide tracks on which different forms, lengths, and heights could be placed. You could have a two-story, three-story, or four-story space of any length, according to the functional need.

The headquarters building is about one kilometer long now. There is a very strong allusion to the prairie architecture of Frank Lloyd Wright, but I had to synthesize this into a system that would work.

I tried to rearticulate the details in a manner different from Wright's. My copings are metal instead of brick. Instead of an all-copper roof, there is lead-coated copper on the overhanging roof and standard green copper on the upper section.

I incorporated similar linear approaches to master planning at Tougaloo College in 1965 and to the Vocational Technical Institute in 1967. Seen in relation to these projects, Domino's is a viable and understandable segment of my design life.

Frank Lloyd Wright, dead since 1959, was respected, but not resurrected. As long as Domino's stayed forty-nine percent Monaghan and Wright and fifty-one percent me, it was all right.

Tougaloo College Camlpus Master Plan, Tougaloo, Mississippi, 1966.

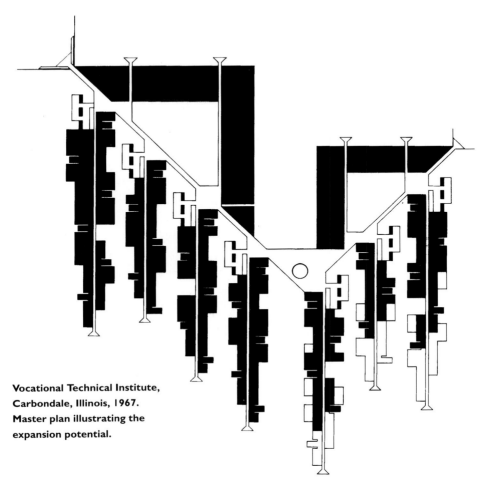

**Vocational Technical Institute,
Carbondale, Illinois, 1967.
Master plan illustrating the
expansion potential.**

Domino's Tower

Domino's tower was a departure I made to get as far away from the Frank Lloyd Wright imagery as I could. It involved the constructivist theory of using dynamic rather than static forces to achieve this departure. Monaghan was convinced that my design conveyed a stronger image than would a recreation of Frank Lloyd Wright's building, the Golden Beacon, to be specific. Personally, I was so disillusioned with my peers for building those funny postmodern buildings that I was anxious to get into structural expression.

There are towers that lean because they are faulty, like the Campanile at Pisa, dangerously close to tipping over now but definitely one of the remarkable buildings in the world. There are towers that lean deliberately, like the dynamic tower Vladimir Tatlin designed for the Third International in 1920. Tatlin and the other Russian constructivists were looking for an expression that didn't perpetuate bourgeois architecture in any form—Classical, Baroque, Romanesque, Bauhaus, or anything else. They wanted to express their own socialist beliefs. But how can you do new architecture with the same old principles?

In the 1980s with Monaghan's tower, I faced the same problem that Tatlin had. It's not so easy to beat the Classical or Romanesque. The way I did it was to challenge some common beliefs about architecture and gravity. I had to challenge gravity in order to depart from the mundane high-rise towers that proliferated from one end of America to the other.

When you analyze the structure, it is really very simple. It's just a leaning truss. There's no trickery in it—just fairly typical engineering calculations. It leans fifteen degrees out of the vertical and there was absolutely no problem in doing that. The biggest problem was what to do with the elevators. I was struggling with having the elevators go up so far, then making people change elevators at a certain floor and go up again. Finally we managed to run an elevator all the way up.

The tower has a very strong and dynamic effect on the viewer. You feel the kinetic force that connects the top and bottom. Being near it is an interesting experience. When I was away in Europe, Mr. Monaghan decided to find out how it would feel and he ordered a model to be built at one-tenth actual height.

I don't consider the tower a turning point in my career. Instead, it was my way of counteracting the Frank Lloyd Wright influences of the headquarters building.

There is a very precarious balance between one's desire and opportunity. If I have been dammed up, and by that I mean that I have not designed lately, I have an enormous urge to design. When given the opportunity, I may shoot from the hip—right into my foot. I may misjudge things because I am so bottled up emotionally. I think architects need a great deal of self-control and maturity not to take their next project and give it all they've got, everything they have dammed up for years. One feels like a vacuum—so much is coming in for so long and then you are poked, and you explode. That's a danger we have to be wary of.

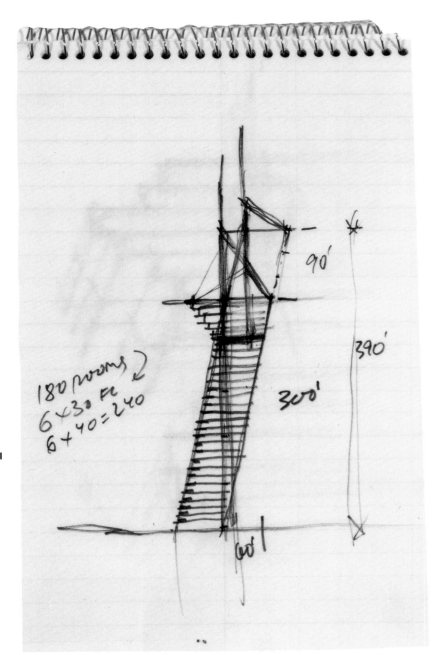

Developmental sketches for Domino's Tower, 1987.

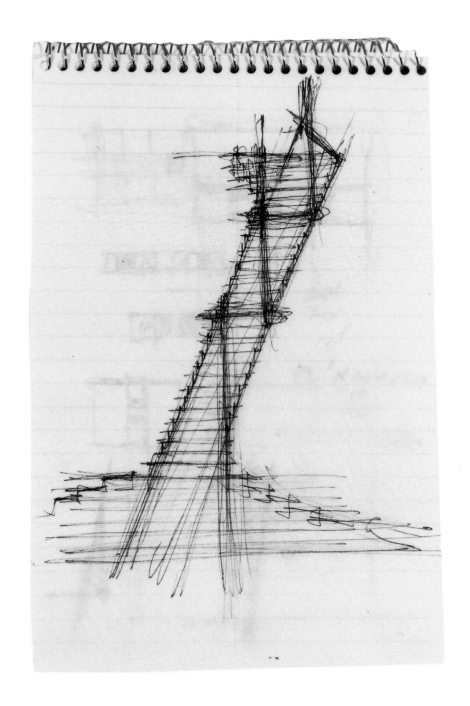

Marge House

Let me tell you how I got the job of designing the Marge house. It is located on Drummond Island in upper Michigan. The owner is a lady who asked me to stay as far away as I could from Frank Lloyd Wright. She couldn't stand him anymore. Well, I could understand that because her husband is Tom Monaghan.

As Tom became more devoted to Frank Lloyd Wright, Mrs. Monaghan became absolutely overwhelmed and disinterested in Wright. She asked me to do a house in which we totally forgot about him. When she asked for this departure she was ready for anything—and so was I. So we did it.

I found the solution by working with sculptural form. This was another case in which the input from the client was so strong that I was in danger of eating my words and going against my belief that it was dangerous to work with the ungenerated form.

I had to see how we could generate the form. We have the house responding to the lake, hiding from the neighbor, and responding to the road. Metaphorically, I see the house as a big boulder, a natural form that will be clad in copper on the outside and wood on the inside. Let's call the house an organic expression.

But on the inside, it has a rather orderly orthogonal plan. The house is a departure because it does not allude to any particular direction in architecture.

This was a very difficult task for me. You can stay away from the forms of Wright, but how can you stay away from his principles? His architecture is at the root of all architecture, in a way. When you talk about organic architecture, he is always there.

The Client as a Committee

Sometimes you have to negotiate with many people at the same time—even with yourself. You take the diverse ideas of the group and work with them to find an answer. Sometimes you find yourself presenting several solutions before you get it right.

You have to educate the client. Look very carefully at the credentials and backgrounds of the people on the building committee. Pay particular attention to the backgrounds of those who don't seem to be accepting your proposal. You find out why when you look deep enough.

Keiichi Miyashita

G. Birkerts

Marge House model, 1989, designed for the wilderness of Drummond Island, Michigan. A rock metaphor suggested the building's form.

But sometimes the best thing to do is step back and allow the group to educate itself. If two members disagree with the proposal and four like it, let the four work on the other two. Give your four friends on the committee enough backup information so they can convince the others.

I like to make clients part of the design process. I don't try to save them from going through it. When the clients are included in the process, I usually get much farther than I would have if I had walked in, pulled the wrapper off a built model, and hoped that everyone thought it was wonderful.

At first I might win acceptance with the model because what I designed was a startling thing, or something that excited the imagination. But after a couple of days, the phone would start to ring. The client has a few questions. Someone says that so-and-so doesn't like the plan anymore. If the clients had been included throughout the process, they would have been part of the creation, and the questions wouldn't be coming now. No one would have been surprised.

In order to start the process, the client gives me the program—what is involved in the spaces and other quantitative factors. The next step is defining the qualitative program. My associates and I discuss with the clients their expectations and how they see themselves. We ask many questions and get the viewpoints of the owners and users.

This is where the concept is really born, during this kind of interaction, assuming that the architect already has an understanding of the site, region, and all the other external and technical factors.

I don't suggest you do this necessarily if you're designing a warehouse or gas station. But such interaction is vital if you are building something that will have great importance to the community, function as a monument, or be a highly visible building that has a philosophy behind its existence.

I am not afraid to show the first conceptual sketches to the client but I would not devote an entire meeting to them. That would only frustrate the client. Nonarchitects will not see in a conceptual sketch what I might see. To them, it might look more like a blob than a building, but to me it contains all the ingredients.

Next is the schematic development of the conceptual sketch. Spatial arrangements and site considerations are brought to the level where they can be discussed. At this point I try to keep the third dimension out of it for awhile, unless it's absolutely necessary. The important thing is the two-dimensional arrangement.

A section of a building is also extremely important in many instances. Sometimes the entire concept of a building is in the vertical arrangement of space in three dimensions. If that is the case, I might present a section and a plan and allow time for the client to perceive the total development. Then I ask for an endorsement of what I have done. Am I right in the spatial arrangements, and is this section through the spaces reflective of our discussions? After I receive the acceptance, then I am free to conceive.

The truth is that I already have a concept, but it is not fully manifested. The work we do up to this point serves to trigger questions from the client, or to help me develop the concept that my intuition already says is there.

While doing the U.S. Embassy in Caracas, Venezuela, I was trying to disguise the building as a form that was part of the geography and geology there. I saw the building as an element being pushed into the mountain rather than projecting from it. The building and the mountain had to be integrated.

I am not afraid to show the first conceptual sketches to the client but I would not devote an entire meeting to them. That would only frustrate the client. A nonarchitect will not see in a conceptual sketch what I might see. To them, it might look more like a blob than a building, but to me it contains all the ingredients.

I cut a section and explained to the client that there would be a blank wall against the mountain and some earth cover where the building entered the mountain. If the client didn't want any part of the building to be buried in the mountain, then I would have known not to go any farther with that idea.

But it worked. The client didn't want fenestration on the back side anyway, yet he wanted to look out from the other side and see the views. At that point, the client didn't know what the building looked like, but he approved the concept. Then I could open up and visualize the rest of the design with greater confidence.

The next step in the process is the formal presentation. It is inevitable that since buildings are three-dimensional creatures, we have to work in the third dimension for the client. In my office, the project architect builds the model, usually of cardboard or foam board. If the form is so sculptural that the model is difficult to adapt during the design process, we use plasticine. Cardboard and foam board are only useful for developing straightline geometry. They are handicaps when you go into another geometry.

Sometimes at this stage I find that the client may not be in agreement with the design once he sees it in three dimensions. This usually doesn't happen because the client has been taken through the logic of the process, but sometimes, there is a setback. Maybe the form is jarring or startling, or for some other reason is not appealing to the client.

Usually within the concept, if it is a good concept, I still have room to make changes. But if the client completely rejects the idea, I try to take the setback as a positive development. Now I really know what the client wants, or what the problem is.

Here comes a big disclaimer: I claim that I can conceive only after I know everything about the project. If I find that I am saturated to the point where I am uninterested and can't hear anymore, then I know that I am filled to my capacity and soon will know the answer. But if the client doesn't like the concept, that tells me that I didn't know everything. I didn't ask enough.

So we go through the entire process again, but it's faster this time. Often it turns out that there was just one ingredient that didn't come up in the discussions. I always want to ask why I wasn't told about it in the first place, but I don't.

Such an ommission can occur when clients have trouble expressing themselves and can only react to what they see. This is common. At this point, many architects might try to mesmerize the client so that everything goes ahead as planned anyway. But in my office, we try to get the truth out of the client as much as we can.

The next step is to make an all-encompassing presentation. It consists of plans, elevations, sections, and models. We very seldom do perspectives.

On the more pragmatic side, there is the cost estimate. The estimating process never stops during the life of the project. In the drawing stage, there are usually three estimates. One is at the beginning, when we don't even know what the building will look like. It's based on typology and a general idea of what the client wants to attain. The other estimates occur during design development and before the start of the working drawings.

Design development does not mean that the design will get changed. It means that the design will be explained and further developed. Concept sketches are usually not more than one-eighth inch in scale. Next we get into quarter- or half-inch scale drawings. These are the drawings that develop spaces and larger sections of the facade.

We address the choice of materials and how the technology is to be incorporated. Another way of saying it is that now we determine what a line in the drawing represents in terms of materials. For example, a particular line might translate into an aluminum mullion holding a two-pane insulating glass section in place with certain gaskets. Suddenly these little things become factors.

During the process of design development we anticipate what will happen in the working drawing phase. We completely design the wall. There is an architect on my team who is a genius at the technology of building enclosures. Designing the building's skin is a very difficult task because this is where architects have the most liability and grief due to problems that develop in the sun, under the pounding of rain and snow, and in extreme temperatures. Skins will always work themselves into oblivion if you don't anticipate the problems.

In design development we also address interior details. Again we make presentations to the client. We introduce materials, colors, and many other things. We begin to address the question of the furnishings that are part of the building and those things that are part of the furniture and fixed equipment budget.

Clients may take months to make up their minds about these details. At Duke University, the law school building went through three different granites—pink, brown, and gray—over the period of a year. Each choice had an effect on the interior scheme. It was a taxing situation.

During the construction phase, the specified materials are submitted by the general contractor for our approval. All the materials are laid out and we approve the stone, the way the glass is put together, the way the wall section is developed. We are very meticulous about this and sometimes ask for a full-size mock-up of the actual materials to be erected by the actual suppliers. Maybe the mock-up is one bay wide and two stories high.

You see, a building is not like a car. Car designers working in a research development department can pound on the design for three years before they put the car on the road. They work out every detail on a single prototype and then they build them by the thousands. But a building is one-of-a-kind. After doing one you usually throw away the mold. Even if you have developed a good skin detail that could be used again, it it likely to change its spots somewhere along the line on the next job.

THE CONTRACTOR AND TECHNOLOGY

A particular folklore surrounds my firm in the contracting community. This does not necessarily work in our favor when it comes to having our work bid upon because the contractors know we insist on specific standards of workmanship and interpretation of our drawings. The ones who know us best include what they call the "Birkerts factor" in their bids and, unfortunately, they bid higher. Then the contractors we haven't worked with before might get the job because their bids are lower. When that happens, we are saddled with the education and surveillance of the new contractors and the enforcement of quality on the project.

When we're working with a new contractor, we overextend ourselves on the drawings. At least then we can put in the drawings and specifications what we intend to achieve. We have special requirements for finishing drywall, concrete finishes, and board forms. We may include a few more details than normal, such as joint alignments, locations, and other relationships that normally would fall within a standard system. But we say we want them our way.

On a simpler job, we may ask the contractor to lay up block or brick and then we take a look at the joints. For sandblasted surfaces, we will ask for a sample and then demand that it is used as the standard for the entire job.

But sometimes we are put over the barrel, too. If my field supervisor comes back to the office and says that a sandblaster sneezed and blasted a streak into the concrete, we cannot tell the owner to tear down the building. Some mistakes are beyond repair. Those you just have to live with.

We have had good luck with contractors in general, mostly because my team is in weekly contact with them. When contractors realize that you care, and when the people actually doing the work realize this, they do a better job. Getting involved with the workers is the best quality control device there is.

Imagine that you are a bricklayer and you're working on a shopping center wall that's 1,000 feet long. Every day all you do is lay so many bricks and nobody cares how they look. But what if you're laying a wall that curves, or does something else, and there is this architect hanging around because he cares about the joints? Well, that becomes another situation.

You may go to the job site on a given day and tell the mason that you want the horizontal joints raked and the verticals flush. You explain that you're after a horizontal expression and you want the depth of the rake to be consistent. Some masons might look at you as if you were crazy, but a good one will make a tool, show it to you, and say, "I'm going to use this to try to get what you want. Is this OK now?"

On the other hand, if a contractor can prove that I'm asking for the impossible, then we have to find out what is possible. We learn all the time. And there are so many new materials on the market that the learning doesn't stop.

We have always been most interested in glass and sealants. Of course, present-day granite and marble surfaces may be only a quarter-inch thick and you can build buildings with laminated panels of marble and insulation. Things used to be much thicker. Still, we like to do a solid granite building.

Years ago we jumped on new products quite quickly. Some of the products that were staples in the '60s and '70s are proving that they were not thoroughly tested. Laminated panels with aluminum insulation are beginning to delaminate. We built a number of buildings with those panels. Discoloration of anodized aluminum is another problem. No one knew how long it would last. That is the problem with high technology.

But you just can't wait around. Sometimes you have to stick your neck out. You could go the old way and just use cotton batting for insulation, but that would stop the advancement of design. From the beginning, my interest was in new materials and new applications.

POSTSCRIPT

When we follow the process of organic synthesis we create expressive architecture. As we respond to space needs we do it without subjecting the solution to inflexible geometry. It is still geometry, but not orthogonal or circular; it is polygonal. Based on polygonal geometry, it is freeform, not organic. Polygonal geometry allows us to express space in form without compromising functional or esthetic considerations. Polygonal form does not "follow function;" it expresses function. There is a difference. Form following function wraps skin around function; form arrived at through organic synthesis responds to both interior and exterior considerations and thus expresses both.

Form following function wraps skin around function; form arrived at through organic synthesis responds to both interior and exterior considerations and thus expresses both.

As the architecture of today is born, it carries within it all of the past, the history of humankind, and the history of building and building technology—it is the background that we inherit. In our lifetimes, we live and educate ourselves, we adopt new developments, we create, and we progress. Our development is based on organic growth principles. It is an evolution, it is a progression, and that is what I believe I am doing. I am growing, evolving in the given time span in which I'm destined to live and be creative.

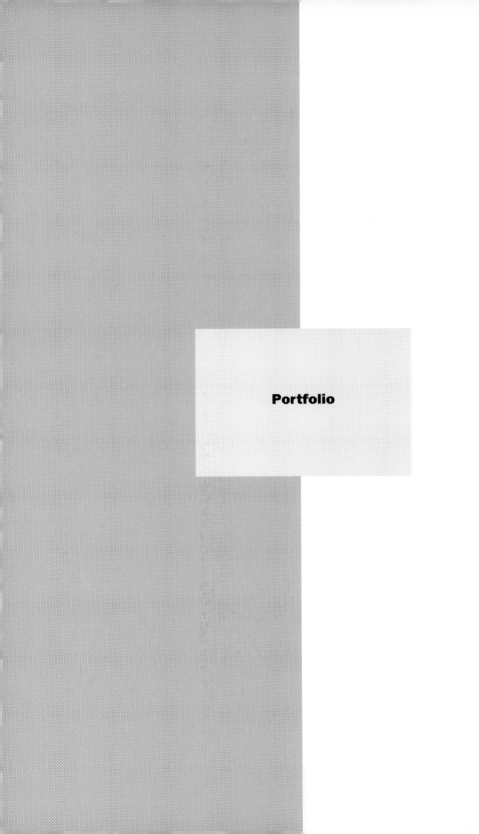

Portfolio

Federal Reserve Bank

Minneapolis, Minnesota, 1968-73

In a capitalist society, the importance of the monetary "circuit" is visible. It is physically expressed by the icons that we build to the system—banks. As the "bank of banks" the Federal Reserve Bank exemplifies this to the highest degree. Given this built-in special status, there was no need for me, as architect, to worry about whether to be modest or not. The decision had already been made.

Balthazar Korab, Ltd.

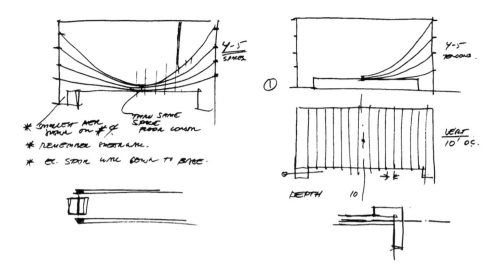

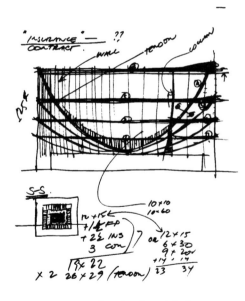

The northern Midwest region of the United States, which this bank represents and services, generated certain kinds of metaphor. The enormous scale of this part of the country—its wide, vast plains, and, further west, its rugged mountain ranges—encouraged the structural module to be bold and the span wide. Further, the geography and climate called forth certain qualities from the people—strength, endurance, and integrity. I tried to express these in the choice of building materials.

The building expressed its inherent functional dichotomy. The fortified, earthy, carved stone base functions to secure the valuables. It is non-communicative and fortress-like. By contrast, the enclosure above is

Conceptual thoughts developed during conversations with structural engineer Leslie E. Robertson. Explorations of structural span options.

transparent, light, and communicative. The two functions, the protective and the administrative, are so different that there was no way to link them structurally into a single form. The dichotomy became a design principle.

The underground area remains secure—there is no structural interference from above, no supports penetrate the surface of the plaza. The upper building is completely sustained by the two major supports, which carry the loads transmitted by the catenary and truss. The bank's structural system had no prototype. No occupied floors had ever spanned eighty-four meters before. In order to get the necessary stiffness, engineers used the full ten-story height of the two side walls as rigid structural frames. Several truss types were considered. The most economical was a braced suspension system. The structural system is clearly expressed on the exterior. The catenary member requires a constant temperature to avoid excessive expansion or contraction and is therefore placed on the inside of the building. The exterior glass skin is in front of the catenary and, after the protection is achieved, it recedes above, expressing the vertical structural system.

The expansion of the building was designed to be on top of the existing structure. The principle employed was the opposite of the catenary—the arch.

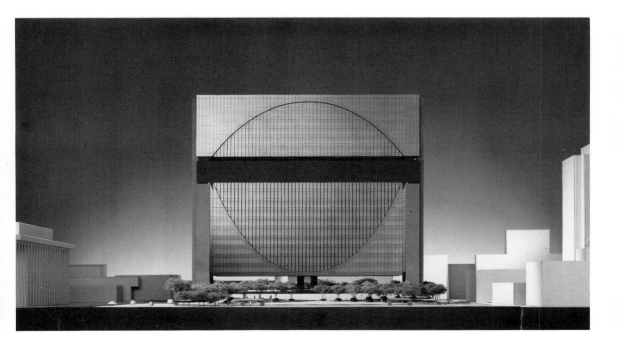

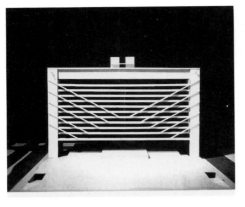 

 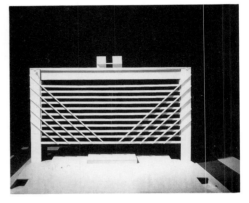

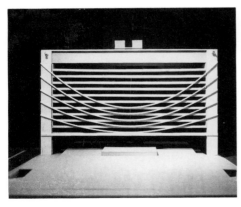 

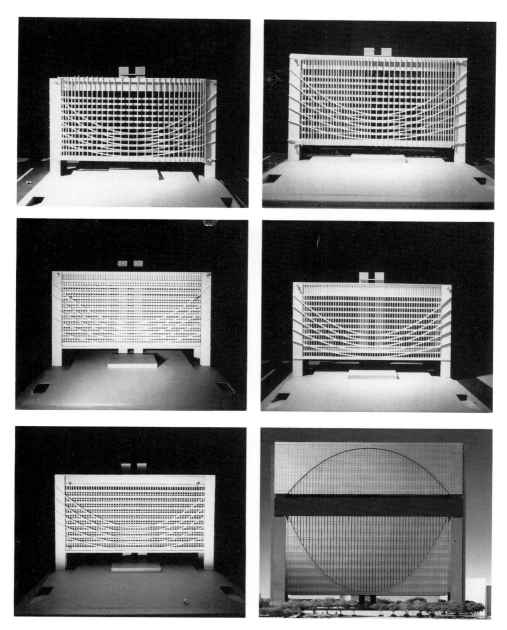

Models of variations in the suspension system of the Federal Bank explored the structural capability of the exterior wall.

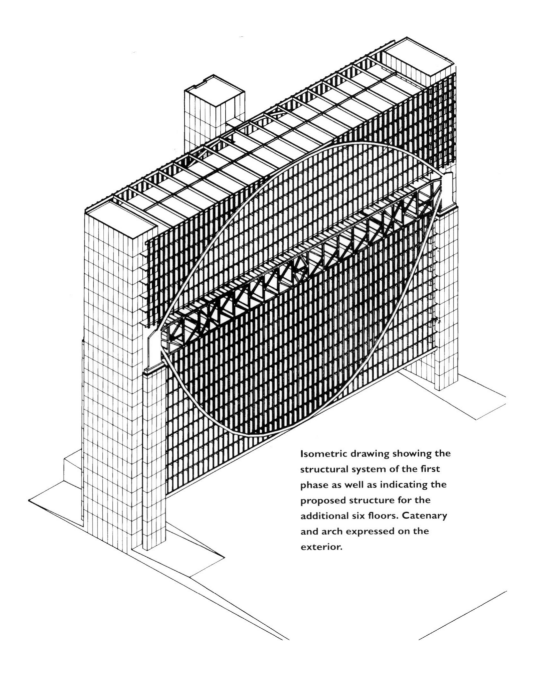

Isometric drawing showing the structural system of the first phase as well as indicating the proposed structure for the additional six floors. Catenary and arch expressed on the exterior.

This construction photo shows the extremely lightweight structural system. One-half of the vertical structural elements are in tension with a very small cross-section. The other (upper) half of the structure is in compression and because of the relatively short length, it also has a small cross-section. The upper truss is not load-carrying and only restrains the end supports against the catenary pull.

Law School Library Addition
University of Michigan
Ann Arbor, Michigan, 1974-81

The Law School at the University of Michigan is a self-contained unit similar to an English college, with its own dormitories, dining hall, library, and social areas. The buildings were built in the 1920s in a pseudo-Gothic style, and the master plan, which occupies a whole city block, had been completed in its final form—with the exception of the southeastern corner. This was to be the site for the proposed addition.

Our office made intensive studies of the functioning of the existing buildings and the effect of a new addition upon them. After a time it became clear that the whole center of gravity for the college would shift if the new addition was built on the proposed corner. We started to search for above-grade schemes that would least affect this center of gravity. A difficult question arose: How do you add a current building to an almost completed architectural presence, particularly when the existing buildings are in the Gothic style? To follow the architecture and the detail of the existing was impossible, or at the very least impractical. The problem of compatibility became quite severe. A contemporary structure hugging the traditional was not acceptable in this case. I began to realize that the only way to go was down.

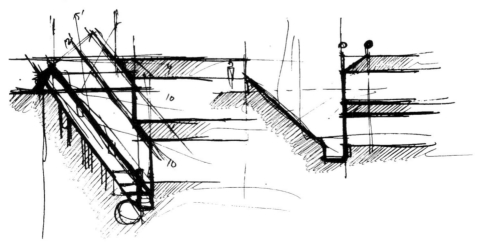

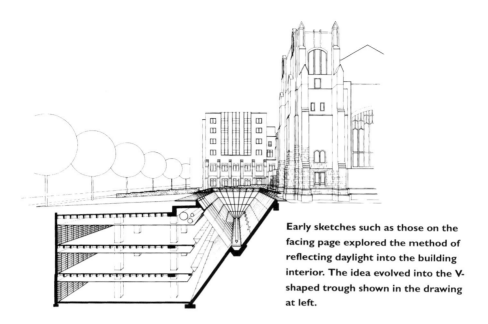

Early sketches such as those on the facing page explored the method of reflecting daylight into the building interior. The idea evolved into the V-shaped trough shown in the drawing at left.

This idea had the support of favorable statistics on energy savings. The possibility of an underground building interested me a great deal. I had been promoting underground structures for many years. The time was finally at hand for the actual implementation of some of my ideas.

My objective was to bring as much daylight as possible into the interior of the underground space, at the same time allowing as much visibility as possible. The plan wrapped the existing library structure and made a connection by tapping directly into the reading room. A deep trough, V-shaped, opens the underground to the outside. The opaque side of the V-shaped groove forms a limestone base for the existing structures but mainly serves to reflect light into the interior of the new space. The glass side of the depressed V-shaped trough allows the underground space access to daylight and an outside view.

The floors, free from the exterior wall, become balconies from which one is able to see out anywhere. The supporting mullions in the glass wall are deepened and covered with mirrors on both sides. The mirrors catch daylight but, most importantly, they help bring in the ambience of the traditional Gothic exterior, its textural detail and coloring, and to increase the feeling of belonging to the above-grade.

66 G U N N A R B I R K E R T S

Museum of Glass

Corning, New York, 1976-80

n the spring of 1976 I was Architect in Residence at the American Academy in Rome. I was familiar with Italy, but four months of uninterrupted stay in the environment of the Academy, where I was surrounded by the vastness of cultural (and architectural) history, was elating. As I look at my work from that time I recognize the visual and emotional influence which my experience in Rome produced.

The Corning Museum of Glass concept was born there. The design was conceived as a flowing extension of the existing Glass Center building. It has a form analogous to that of glass, which is amorphous in the molten state and acquires highly structured crystal properties in the solidified state.

The building's glass skin further reinforces the metaphor established by the form. We developed a new type of glass for this enclosure—patterned sheet with stainless steel coating on its backside. The result is visually rich since, depending on the viewing angle, it projects either the visual quality of glass or metal. To protect the

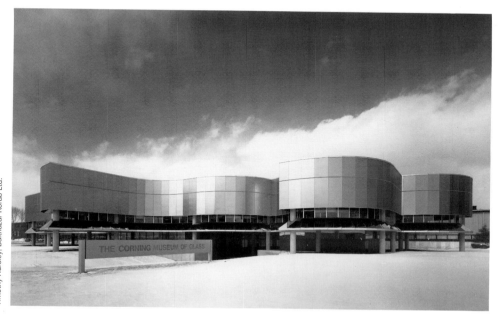

Timothy Hursley, Balthazar Korab Ltd.

exhibit space and the glass objects from incoming ultraviolet radiation, a vision slit is placed below eye level. A system of mirrors arranged at forty-five-degree angles, parallel to each other according to the principle of a periscope, lifts the reflected exterior view above the direct view. The combined images, part real, part illusion, allow for full exterior awareness. The museum exhibition area is lifted above ground to protect the precious contents from possible flood damage. The museum offices, however, are placed under, recessed, and they follow the orthogonal grid of the inner structure.

The exhibition circulation flows clockwise and represents the chronological development of glassmaking. In the Grand Circulation Gallery masterpieces of each era mark the points of highest achievement. For further inquiry, the interested viewer can penetrate more deeply into the exhibit spaces toward the exterior wall.

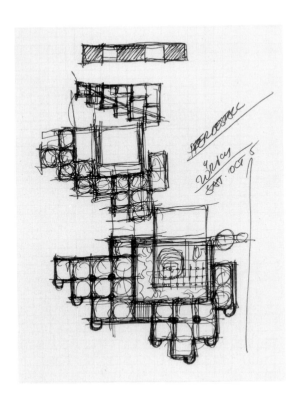
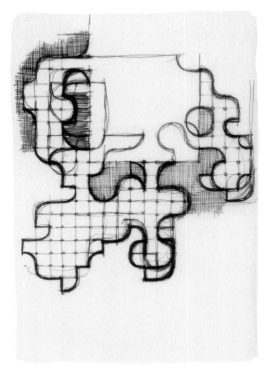

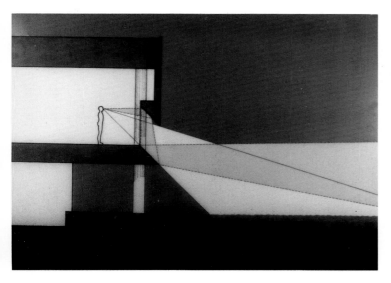

Left: A continuous liner periscope along the exterior wall admits daylight below eye level and allows direct and reflective views to the outside. **Below:** The initial exploration of the building program on site; metamorphosis and the beginning of the concept; a hard line drawing elaborated on the overall concept; a conceptual sketch indicated programmatic zones—library, concourse, and exhibition space.

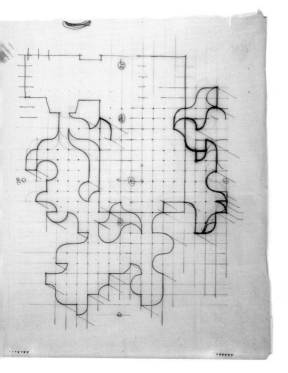

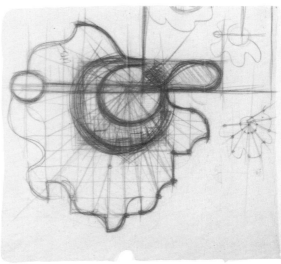

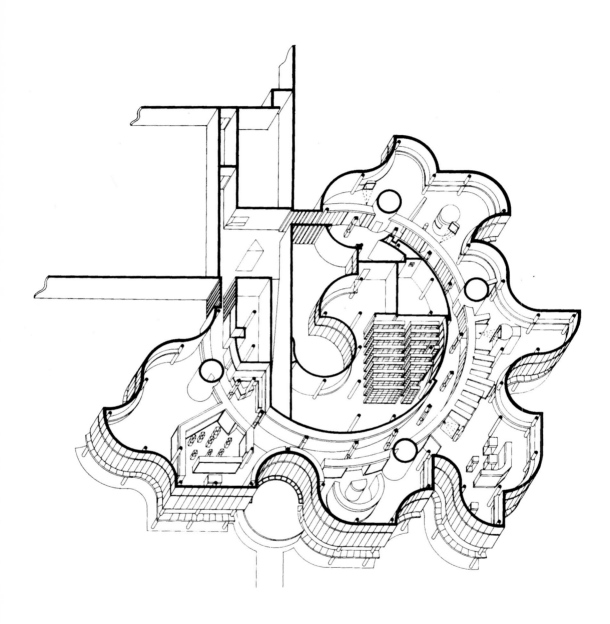

The final layout of the exhibition floor and library, shown in the drawing at left, resulted in the bulding shown above.

Residence

San Francisco, California, 1986

(Project)

A hilltop overlooking San Francisco and the Bay was the setting for this house. Its form was determined by the client's lifestyle and by the surrounding natural environment. In plan it responds to the client's functional requirements. In form it draws from the land nearby and in the distance. In silhouette the house could form the top of the mountain on which it sits. Both form and selection of materials bind the built structure with nature. In a way, this is the precurser to Marge house on Drummond Island, Michigan, and to the Grasis house in Vail, Colorado.

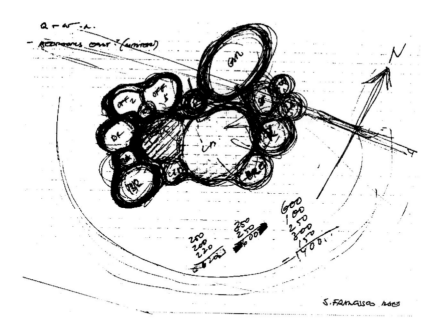

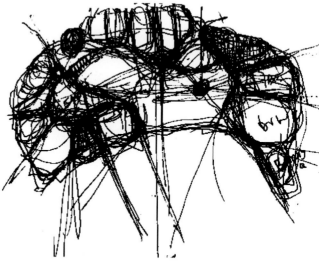

Early sketches explored possibilities for the structure. These drawings explored functioning spaces and orientation.

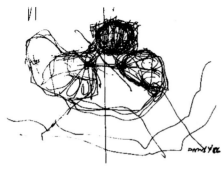

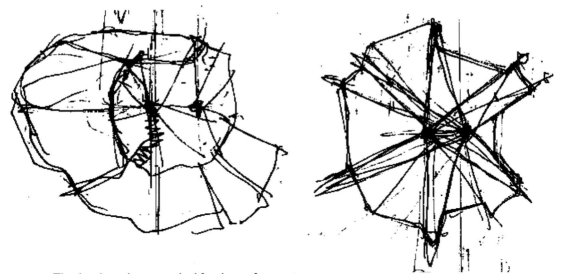

The drawings above searched for the roof geometry.
The sketch below probed the third dimension in
section and elevation.

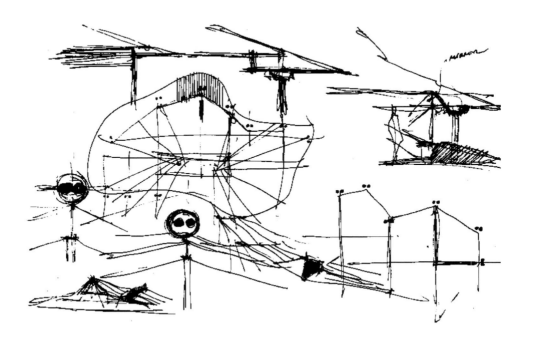

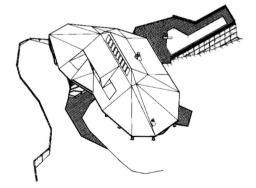

Axonometric (left) and main floor and site plan drawing (below) of the residence.

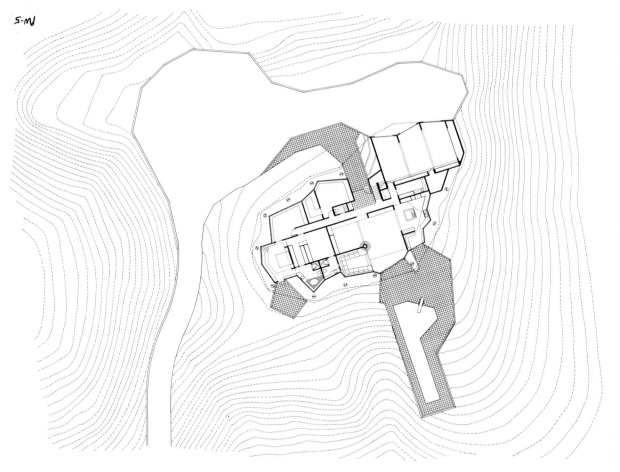

Central Library Addition
University of California, San Diego, 1987-93

William Pereira designed the University of California's Central Library in the late 1960s; its addition was deliberately designed to be subordinate to the strong, geometrical form of the existing building, sited at the head of a canyon near the center of campus. The lower two stories form a pedestal for the six-story stepped tower of this eight-story concrete structure. In the first design concept, the seldom-used open space under the megaform was to become an enclosed, functional interior environment. The three-story addition would have opened to this grand space allowing in daylight and maintaining visual continuity. It was to be earth covered, providing an extension of the campus green cover. This proposal was not accepted and subsequently, a second (and final) solution was presented.

In the second proposal, the addition is placed underground and surrounds the pedestal on three sides. It attempts to remedy the loss to the canyon caused by the intrusion of the pedestal. The canyon is perpetuated by opening the seam between old and new, forming "daylight canyons" which bring daylight into the underground spaces of the addition. Its faceted glass walls, like transparent fault lines in the rock, symbolically refer to the original geological formations of the area.

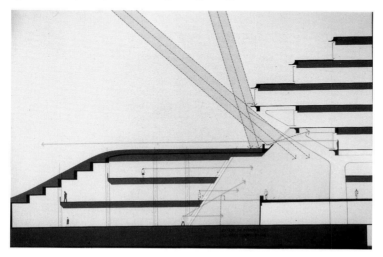

LEFT: **A section drawing, first proposal.**

RIGHT: **A site plan placing the existing building platform in the canyon, extending the canyon walls which ultimately become the enclosing walls for the building itself (final proposal.)**

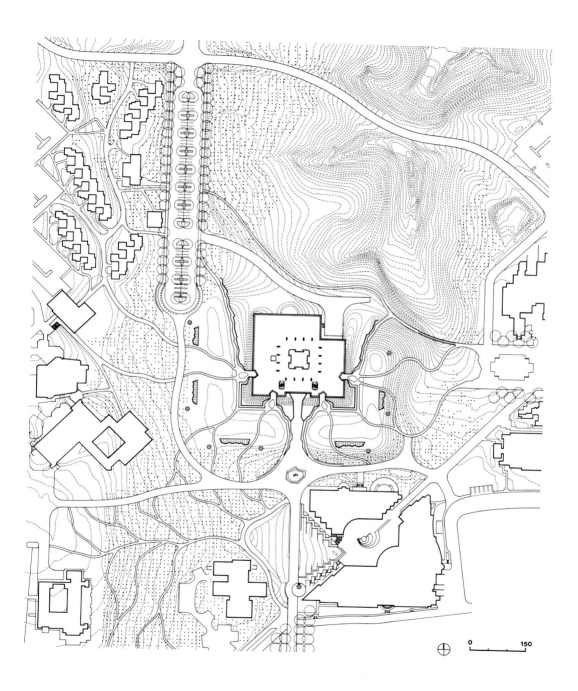

0 150

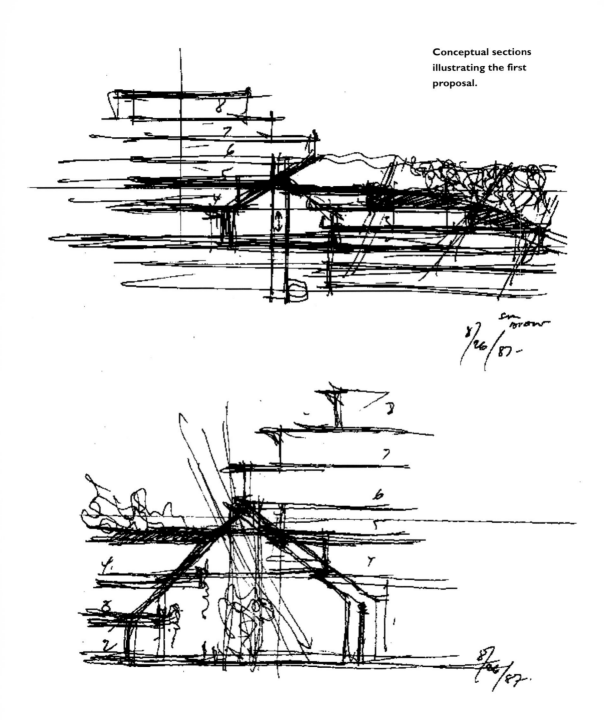

Conceptual sections illustrating the first proposal.

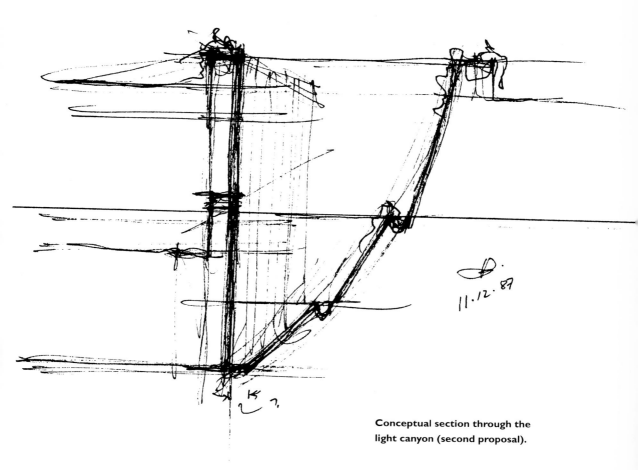

11.12.87

Conceptual section through the
light canyon (second proposal).

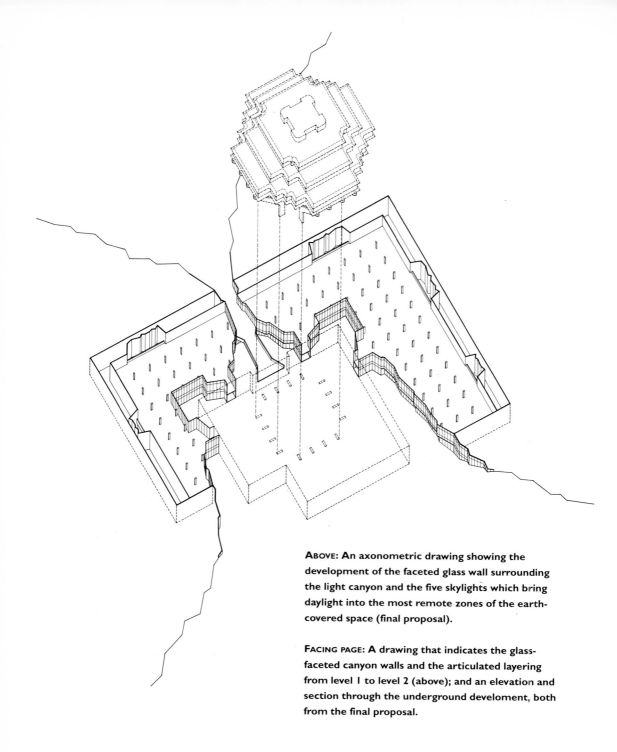

ABOVE: An axonometric drawing showing the development of the faceted glass wall surrounding the light canyon and the five skylights which bring daylight into the most remote zones of the earth-covered space (final proposal).

FACING PAGE: A drawing that indicates the glass-faceted canyon walls and the articulated layering from level 1 to level 2 (above); and an elevation and section through the underground develoment, both from the final proposal.

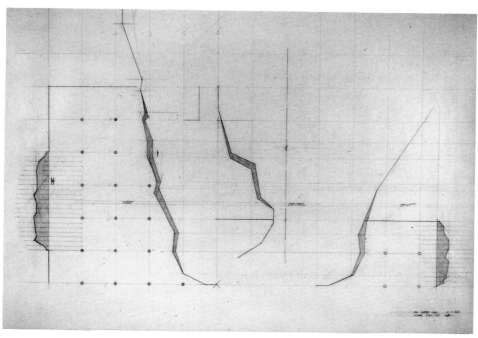

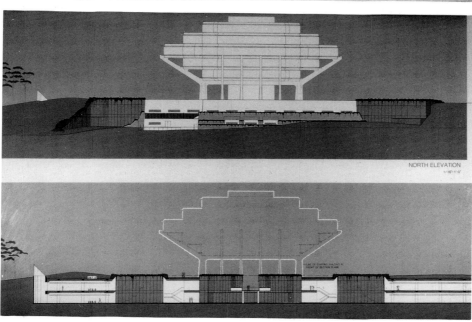

NORTH ELEVATION
1/16"=1'-0"

Law School Addition
Ohio State University
Columbus, Ohio, 1988-93

A second addition to the law school unifies the two existing parts and creates an identity for a new whole. The new building form is generated by its prominent location on campus and by recognizing the limited site and site set-backs. The site is the first view of the campus many visitors will encounter, and as such, it acts as an introduction or gateway to the larger campus beyond; it literally points toward the center of campus—the Oval.

The faceted building form, with its elongated exterior walls, allows ample daylight inside. The pattern of the punctured windows is determined by the amount of light required in certain areas. The limestone and bronze exterior responds to the prevailing campus vernacular and to the existing structure of the law school.

Keiichi Miyashita

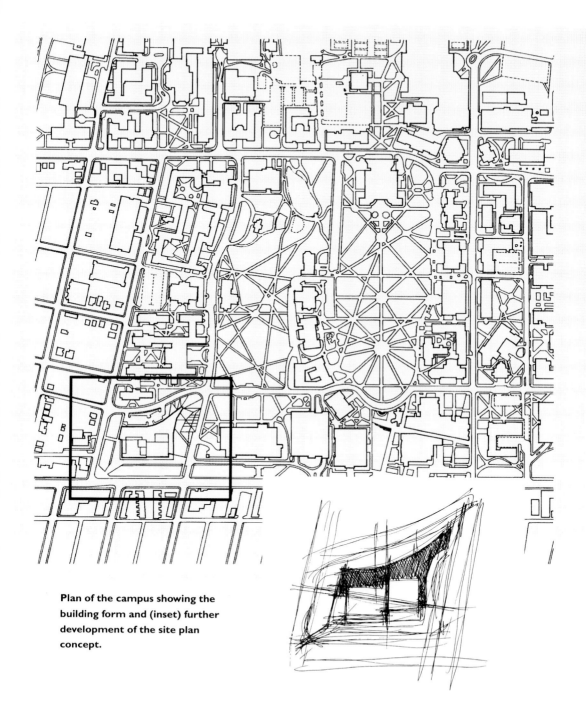

Plan of the campus showing the
building form and (inset) further
development of the site plan
concept.

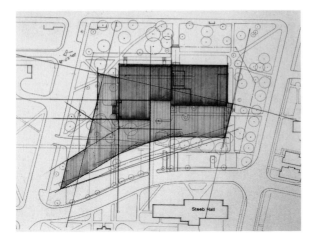

An early site plan concept exploration (left), and the final site plan.

FACING PAGE: An axonometric drawing and plan of the building form.

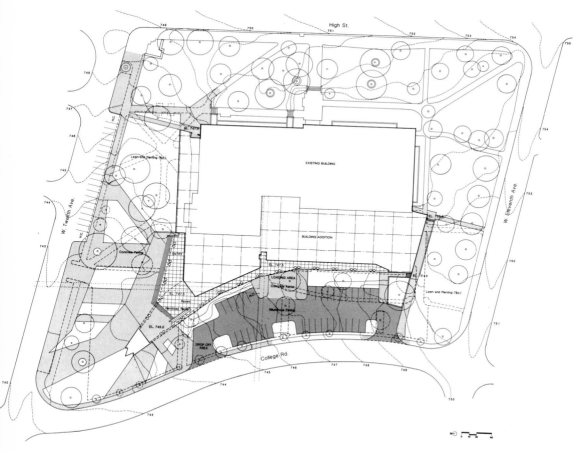

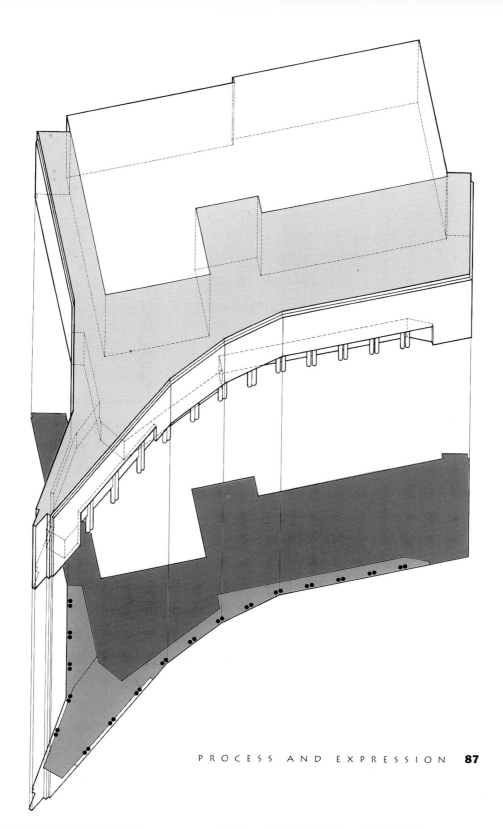

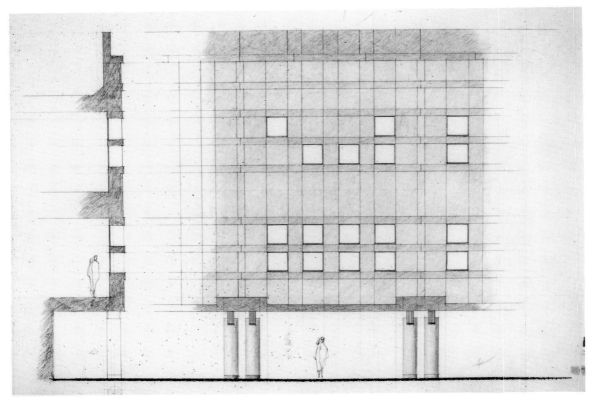

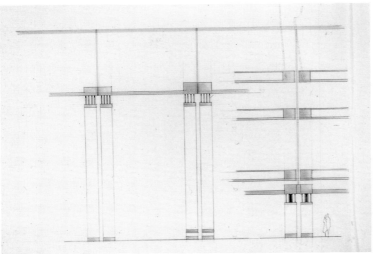

Facade studies.
At right, a detail
study of the
prow and a
partial model of
the building.

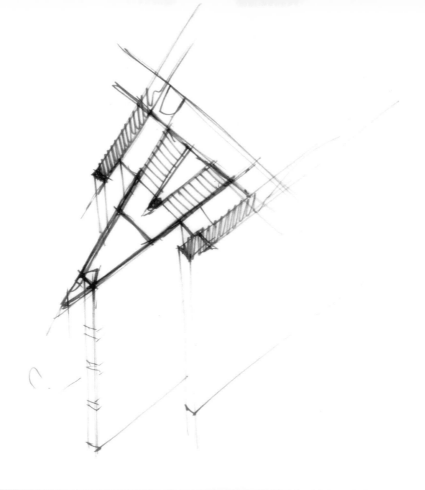

U.S. Embassy
Caracas, Venezuela, 1989
(Under Construction)

Located in the Andean foothills above and south of the Caracas city valley, the site of the U. S. Embassy is characterized by steep slopes and three large plateau areas. The building form responds to the geology of the site, expressing the imagery of the nearby rock formations. In contrast to the surrounding verticality of high-rise office and apartment buildings reaching up from the valley, the Embassy is a horizontal structure stretching across the contours of the site. Three levels are burrowed underground on three sides, with the two upper levels above ground.

Reinforcing the image of the Embassy as part of the mountainside, the faceted front facade is defined by layered overhangs that project outward as the building rises. The structure is of reinforced concrete clad in red granite.

A stone quarry (left) metaphorically influenced the building expression. Below is an axonometric of the building mass with the layering evident in plan and elevation.

FACING PAGE: The building site before construction.

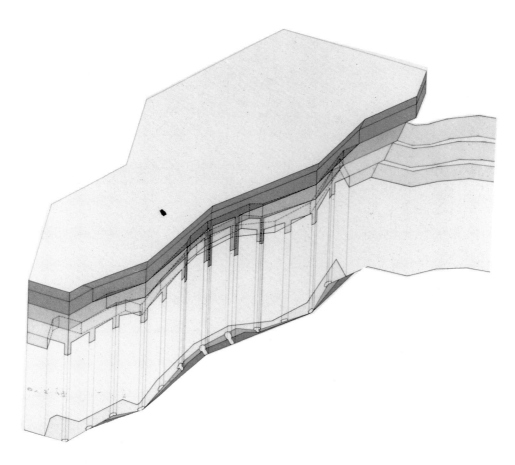

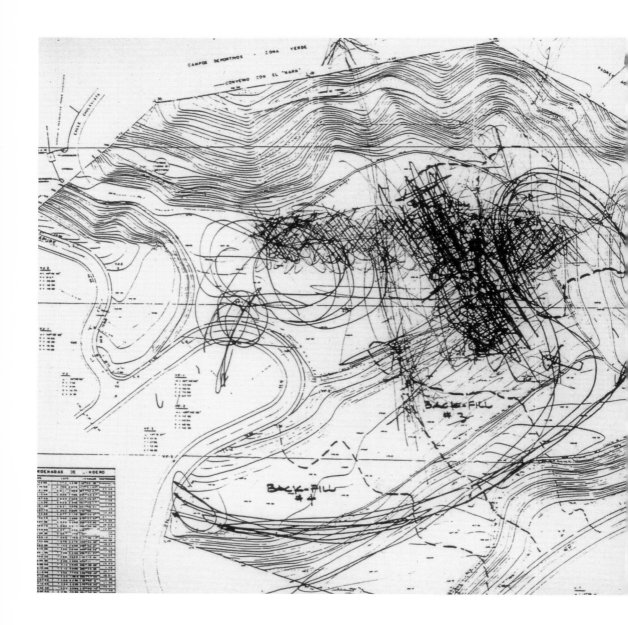

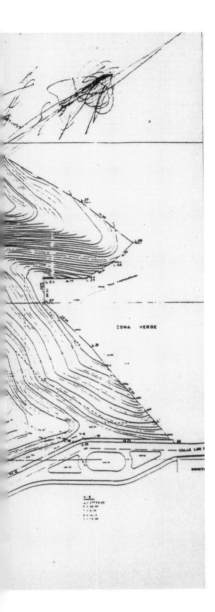

A site plan with study of site access and building orientation.

BELOW AND OVERLEAF: A series of sketches relating the building form to the earth form; the imagery of the layered stone quarry metaphor and study of angle of vision through the enclosing wall.

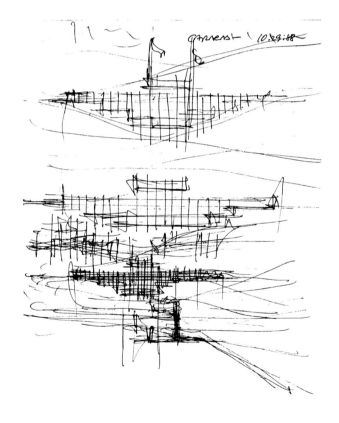

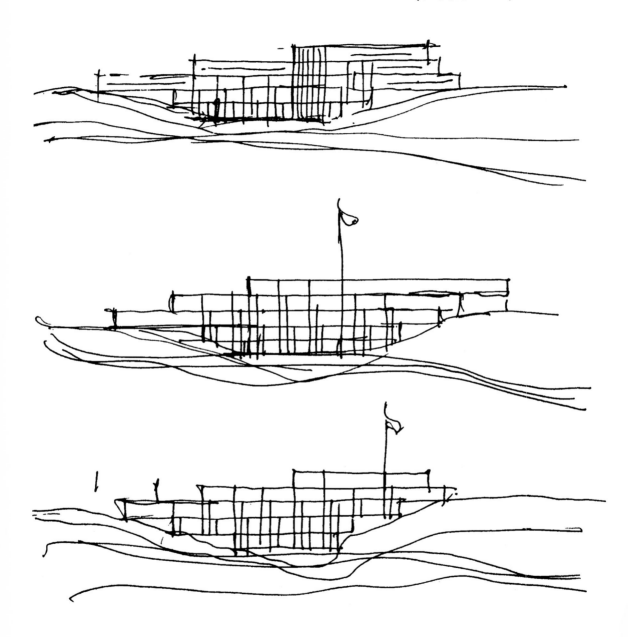

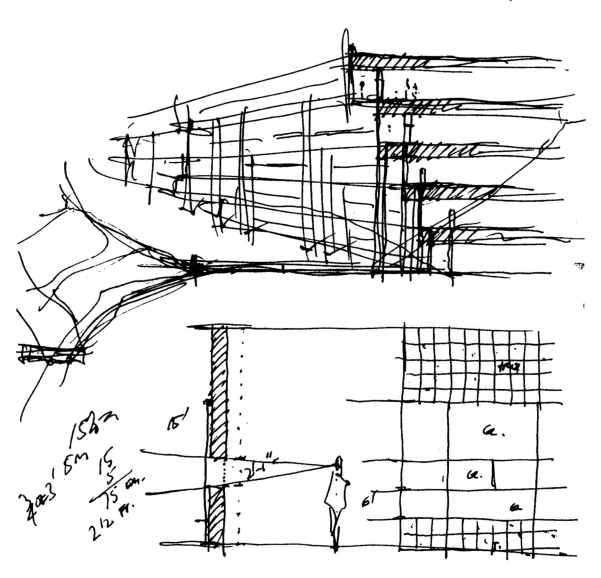

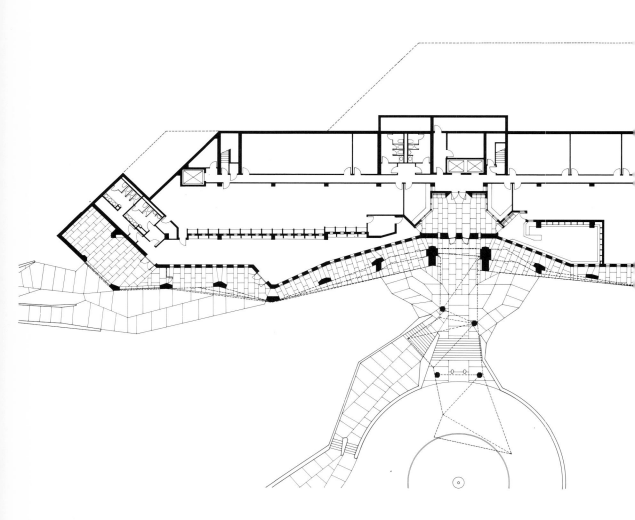

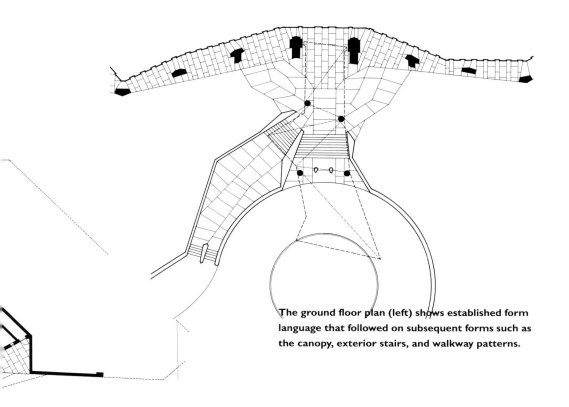

The ground floor plan (left) shows established form language that followed on subsequent forms such as the canopy, exterior stairs, and walkway patterns.

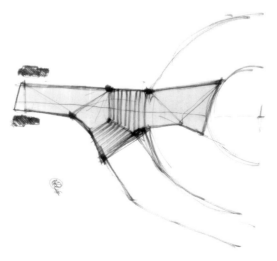

GUNNAR BIRKERTS

Keiichi Miyashita

The form of the walkway and canopy is generated by functional need in all three dimensions.

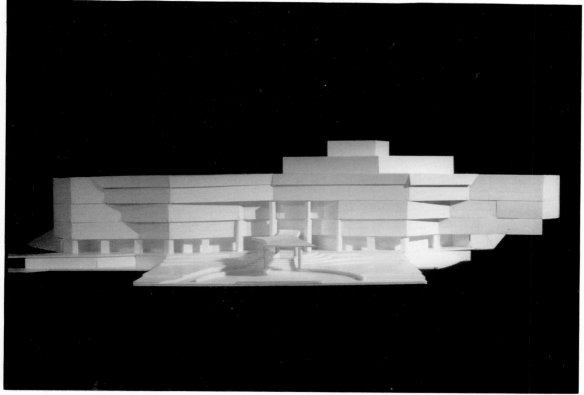

Keiichi Miyashita

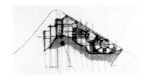

**Humanities Faculties
University of Torino, 1990
Torino, Italy
(Project)**

Given the large scale of the new facility for the University of Torino, urban design considerations were paramount in arriving at a design solution. The design envisions the creation of a major green space, a public park, and an activity zone that connects with existing green zones in the city. The project is located on a sixteen-acre site formerly occupied by the Italgas works in the city of Torino and will include classrooms, seminar rooms, faculty offices, a library, a student activities center, and underground parking.

The proposed urban building forms recognize the scale and vernacular expressions of the existing context. The three-story classroom wing maintains the prevailing street facade imagery with arcaded sidewalks. On the garden side, building forms are polygonal and softer, interfacing with the greenery. The high-rise tower, with offices for administration and faculty, is also expressed in polygonal geometry in its plan. The building acts as a keystone between the academic wing and the student service block. The proposed high-rise is unique for Torino and was the result of the urban planning desire to create a new open public green space.

Keiichi Miyashita

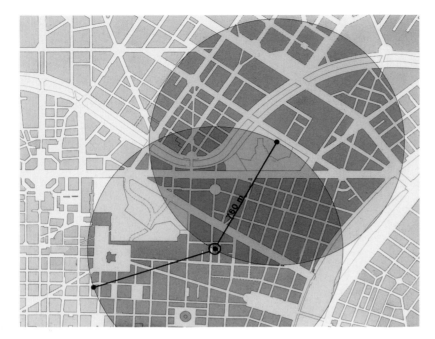

The most important high-rise structure in Torino is the Mole Antonelliana, a symbol for the city. Great care was taken in relating the proposed high-rise office tower to this symbol. It was established that the distance between them was sufficient so their relationship would not be visually incompatible.

Section of the Torino urban plan showing the green space relationship from the Giardini Reali (Royal Gardens) to the project site.

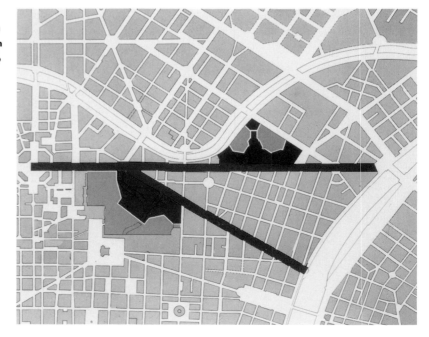

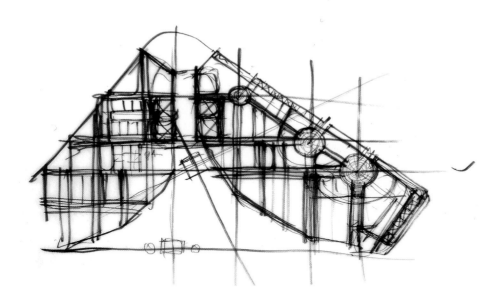

Preliminary
exploration of the
master plan. Some
of the footprints
from the previous
Italgas structures
have remained in
the plan and are
visible as circular
forms.

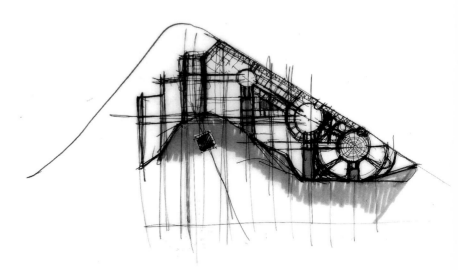

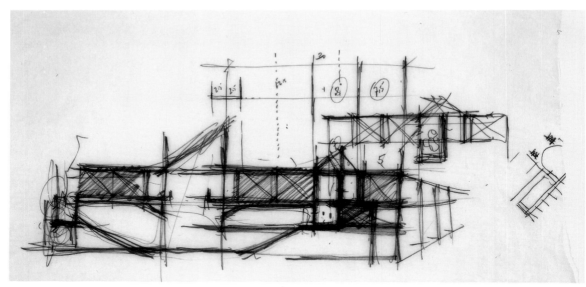

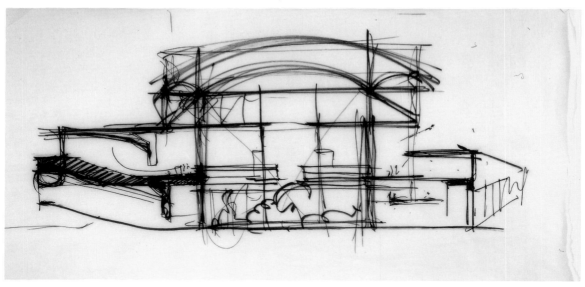

Conceptual sketches of a section through the academic wing show
circulation, auditoria, and seminar areas (above) and auditoria
connecting to the major circulation space (below).

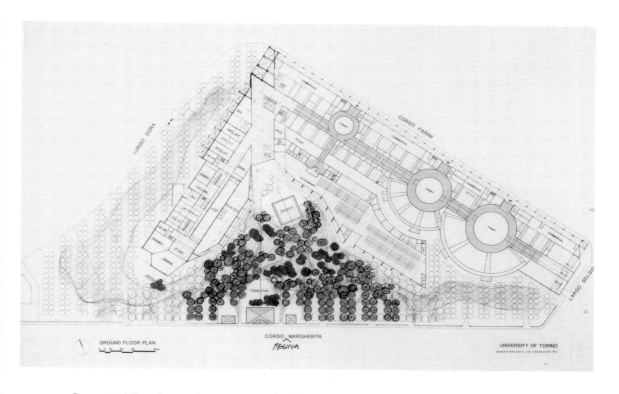

GROUND FLOOR PLAN

CORSO MARGHERITA
REGINA

UNIVERSITY OF TORINO
DUNHAM DINCORTE AND ASSOCIATES INC.

Conceptual thoughts on the green space development.

Below, the ground floor
plan as it was finally
proposed; at right, a site
development drawing
emphasizing the polygonal
form interfacing with the
green space.

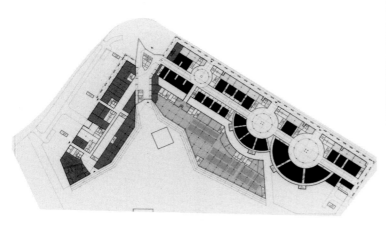

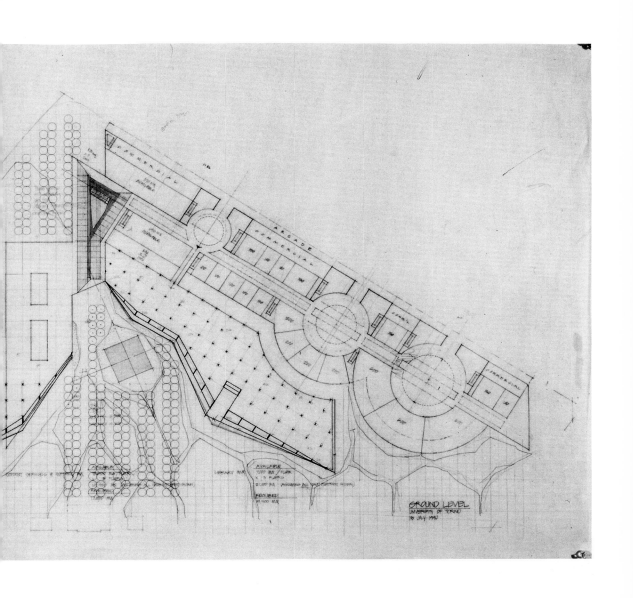

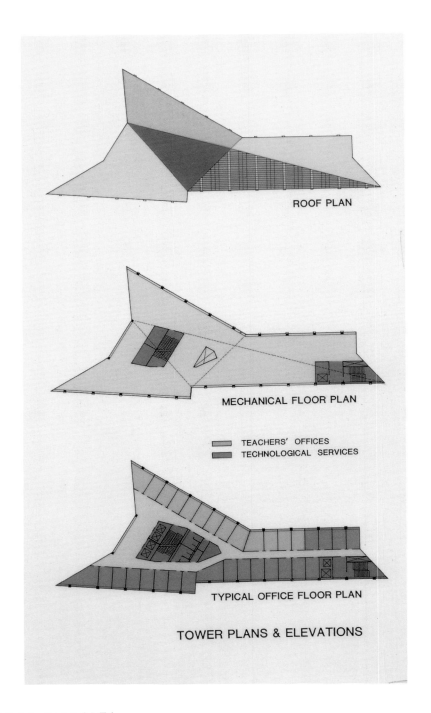

ROOF PLAN

MECHANICAL FLOOR PLAN

TEACHERS' OFFICES
TECHNOLOGICAL SERVICES

TYPICAL OFFICE FLOOR PLAN

TOWER PLANS & ELEVATIONS

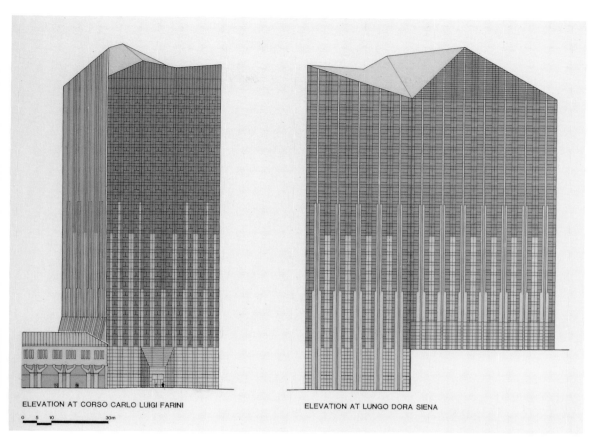

ELEVATION AT CORSO CARLO LUIGI FARINI

ELEVATION AT LUNGO DORA SIENA

0   5   10   30m

ABOVE: A building elevation shows the progression in the use of skin materials. The base begins in stone which interacts with steel above and then glass. The building form ends with glass roof planes recalling the mountain silhouette in the background.

LEFT: The generic American high-rise office structure was not acceptable. The search was made for a form specific to and expressive of the city and this location in particular.

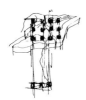

Novoli, Multi-Use Center

Florence, Italy, 1988

(Project)

The scar left by the removal of an industrial sector in the city of Florence will receive a careful grafting of urban development. A mixed-use complex, the development is organized around a new public park in which separate building parcels were allocated to each of seven architectural firms.

Our section of the project is an 865,000-square-foot mixed-use structure that includes office, commercial, and residential space with three levels of parking. The concept form alludes to the scale and texture of historical Florence by clustering offices and housing in articulated masses on a multilayered base. In the base are two parking decks underground and one at street level. The commercial areas, on a platform above the street, parking decks, and the park, are all connected to the surrounding community by cascading stairs and landscaped terraces. The residential complex is composed of three six-story buildings which are oriented toward the central park. The proposal is an integrated, mixed-use concept.

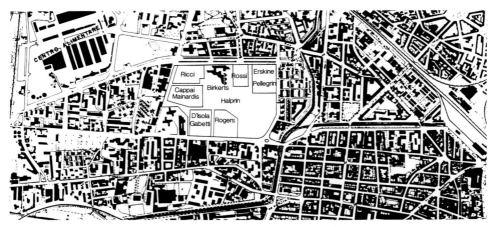

Under Lawrence Halprin's guidance, Cappai & Mainardis, Roberto Gabetti, Aimaro Isola, Luigi Pellegrin, Leonardo Ricci, Richard Rogers, Aldo Loris Rossi, and I worked together within a master plan for the area. The plan is shown above. At right is a typical street in historical Florence.

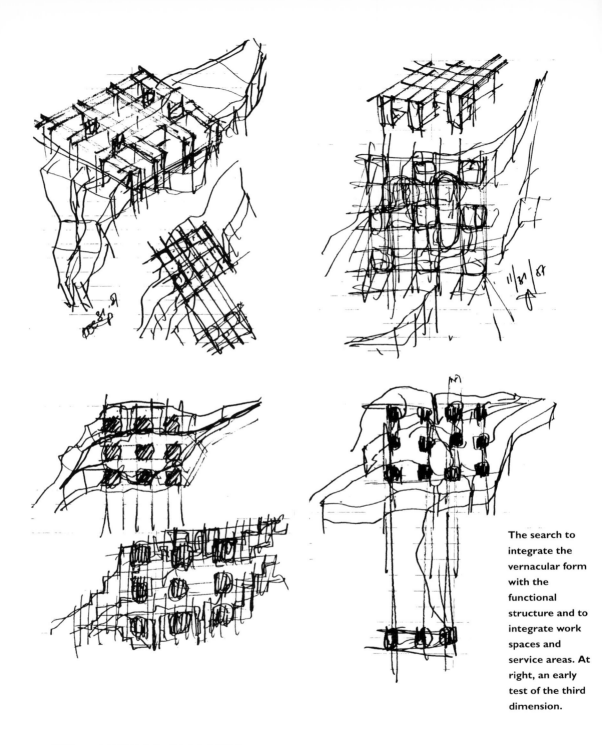

The search to
integrate the
vernacular form
with the
functional
structure and to
integrate work
spaces and
service areas. At
right, an early
test of the third
dimension.

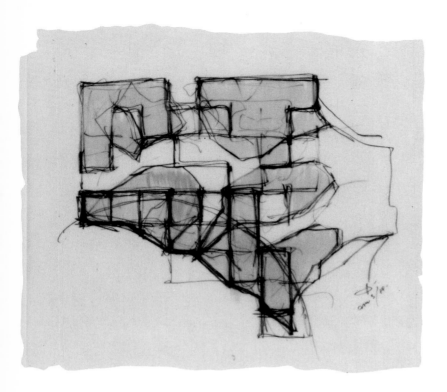

Street level commercial and recreational space development. The office space order visibly affects the plan. Polygonal form response to nature and park development.

FACING PAGE: The commercial level accepts penetration of several cores from above. The polygonal building form is a response to the proximity of the park.

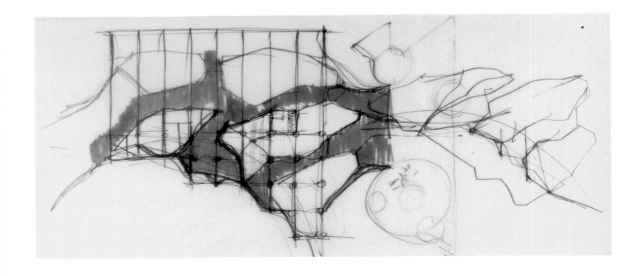

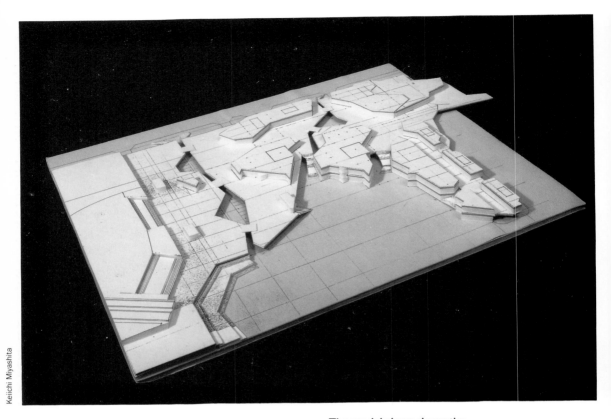

The model above shows the
commercial level with penetrations
into the parking decks. At right,
another model in the series
demonstrates the way in which the
office structure becomes integrated
into the overall form.

Keiichi Miyashita

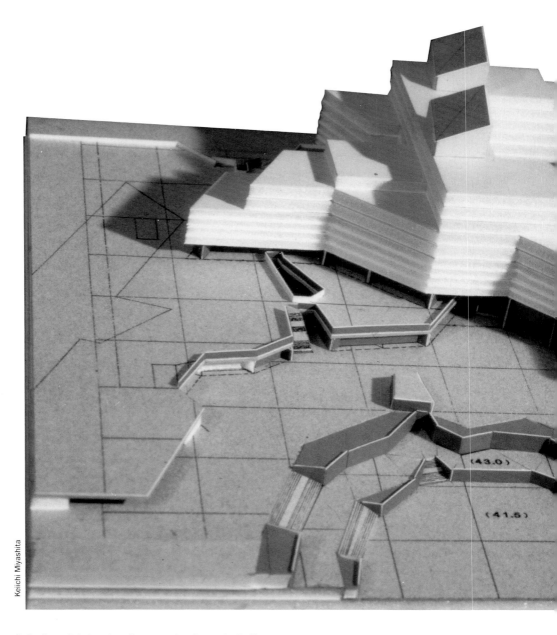

(43.0)

(41.5)

Keiichi Miyashita

A final model showing the terracing from the built portion into the park.

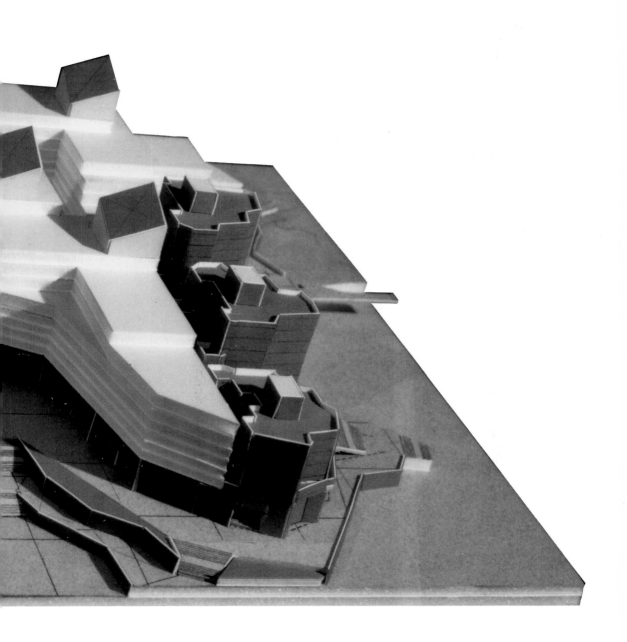

National Library

Riga, Latvia, 1989

(In Process)

Latvia is a small country of great cultural wealth. Its thousand-year history has been carefully recorded in folklore, music, and literature. Because the National Library will become the depository of Latvian cultural materials, the building has to express the country's rich heritage. The building form recalls Latvian fables and poetry, including the folk tale of the Crystal Mountain in which the hero struggles to ride up the mountain to awaken a sleeping princess, an allegory for the country's fight for freedom. The theme recurs as often in Latvian folklore as the loss of freedom occurred in its history. Other stories about sunken castles and fortresses rising out of the dark waters into the sun were also recalled during the conceptual process. The form of the central book storage area evokes the crystal mountain metaphor. It is a faceted linear structure of concrete faced with textured glass. In response to the urban scale and vernacular of Riga, the projecting masonry forms on the side of the glass mountain relate to the scale of buildings across the river to the north and to the proposed cultural center development to the south.

A view from St. Peter's across the River Daugava looking
toward the site (facing page). Above, the city plan of Riga
with site location indicated.

The verticality found in the building forms echoes the typical Latvian white birch groves. The forms of the historical Latvian fortress were also influential in the search for form, particularly for the reading areas of the building that project toward the north.

Klets are historical Latvian farm storage buildings. The organizing logic of the klets was adopted as the organizing principle for the library proposal in which more precious goods are placed on the upper level. Rare books and archives were placed up high due to the potential for a catastrophic flood.

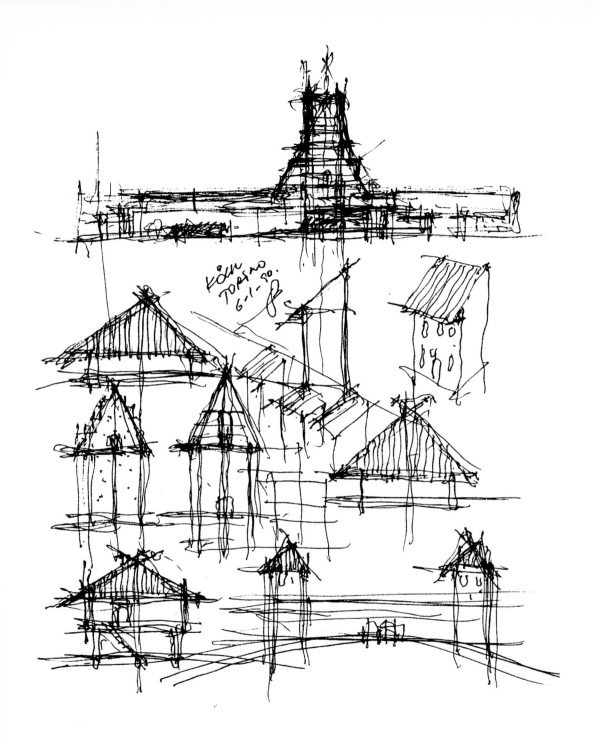

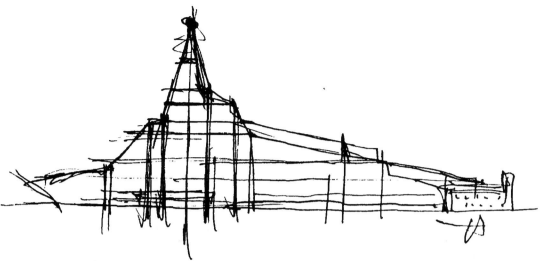

At left, very early explorations recalling historical and metaphorical influences. Above, the first suggestion of the Crystal Mountain metaphor. At right, Sigulda Castle, a strong historical influence and still an important historical artifact on the Latvian landscape, even though it was erected by colonial powers.

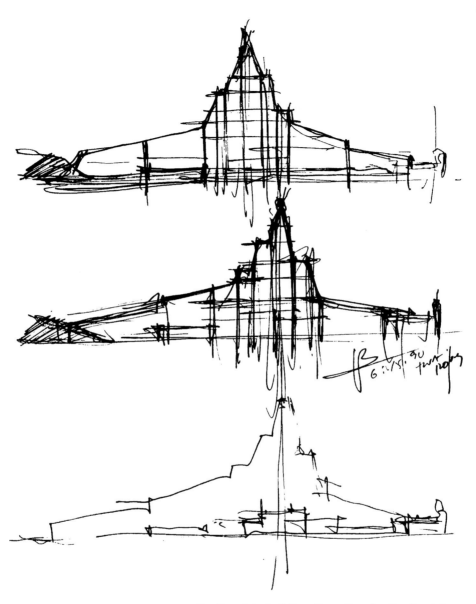

Studies of the building silhouette using the Crystal
Mountain metaphor, above, and a conceptual section
beginning to identify the reading, storage, and work areas
with the first emergence of the atrium space, right.

Sketches showing the three main elements of the proposed building form: urban scale reference to Riga vernacular, mountaintop castle image, and vertical image of the birch grove. At right, facade development studies.

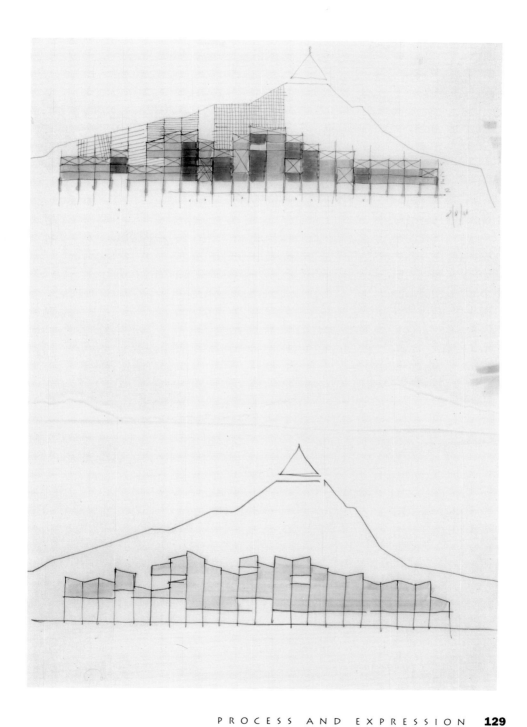

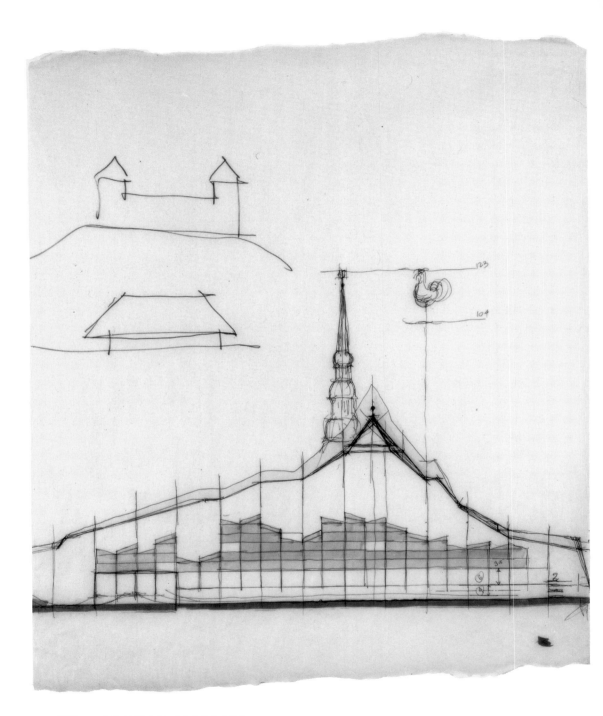

123
104

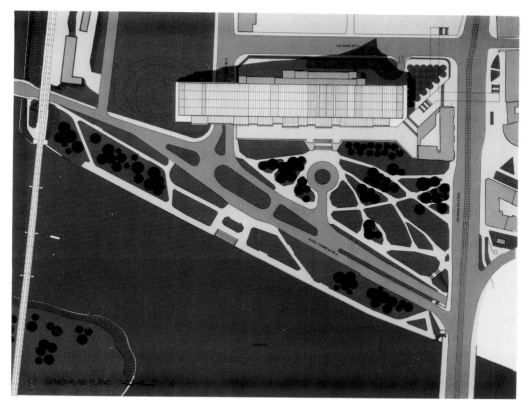

GENERALAIS PLĀNS

At left, a study of the building form and its relationship to the
important historical church spire landmark of St. Peter's, across
the River Daugava. Above, the site plan.

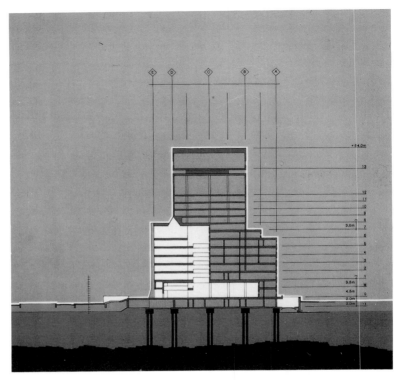

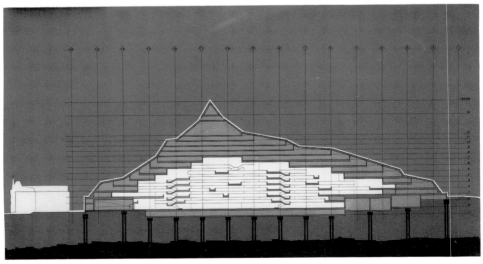

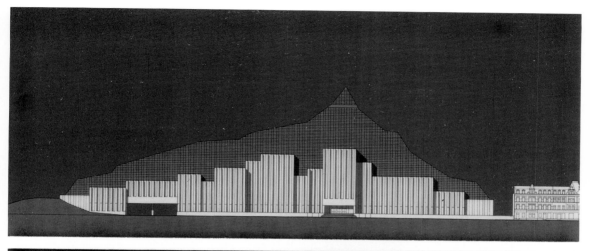

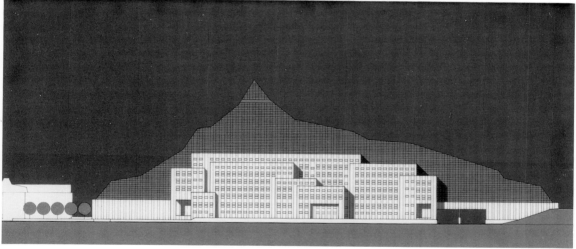

Left, cross-sections showing reading, storage, and work spaces and the central atrium formed by this grouping. The book storage and archival area hovers over the atrium and reading space. Above, the facade facing the River Daugava to the north (top) and the south facade.

Model of facade facing the River Daugava to the north.

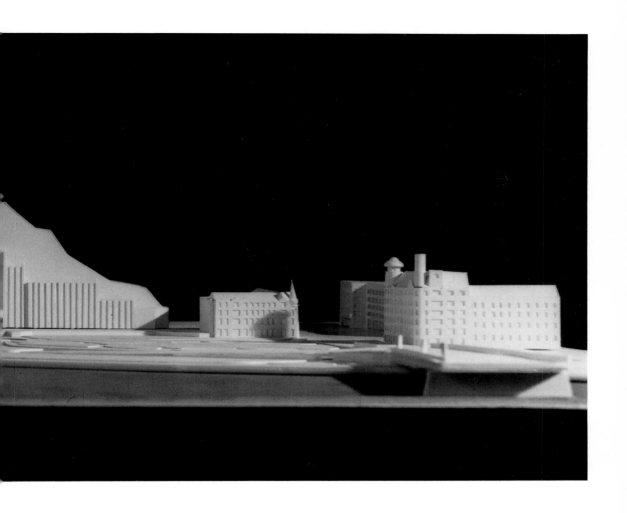

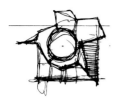

Honors College Building

Western Michigan University

Kalamazoo, Michigan, 1987

(Project)

The building form is extracted from the University's existing, rather eccentric master plan. The master plan's formalized beginning and subsequent unstructured planning became influential in the search for the image of the Honors College. Subsequently, both the orthogonal formal grid and the almost schizophrenic planning approach became expressed in the building form.

A similar search for form was also at the base of the Kansas City Art Institute Kemper Museum of Contemporary Art and Design where the form was a distillation or synthesis of the surrounding architectural vernacular.

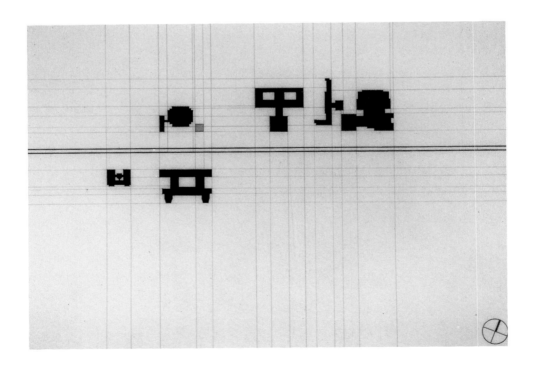

Part of the campus was built in the orthogonal order (facing page) but the overall campus plan showed an unorganized distribution of built architectural form. This became the main ingredient in the concept for the building. An initial concept sketch, left, reflected the architectural vernacular and angular placement of buildings.

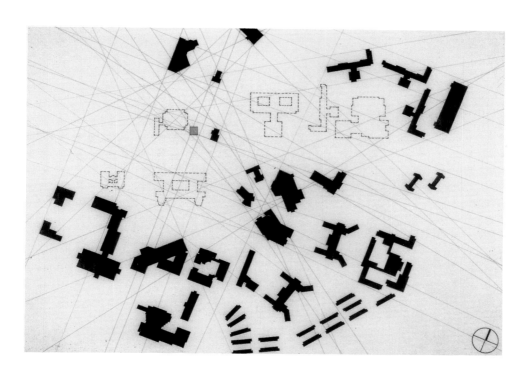

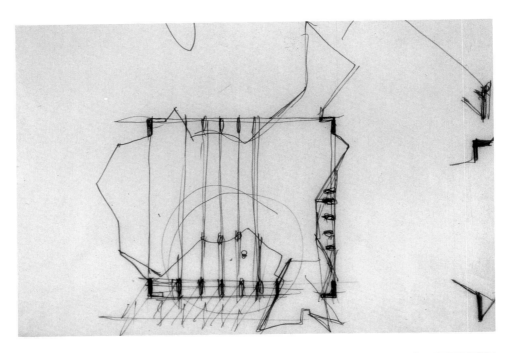

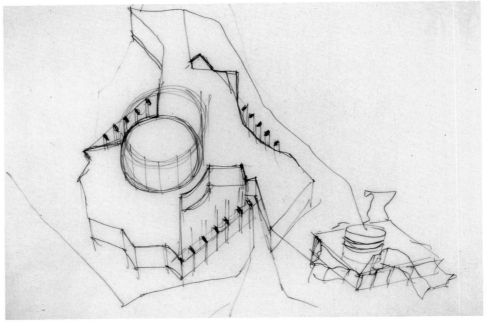

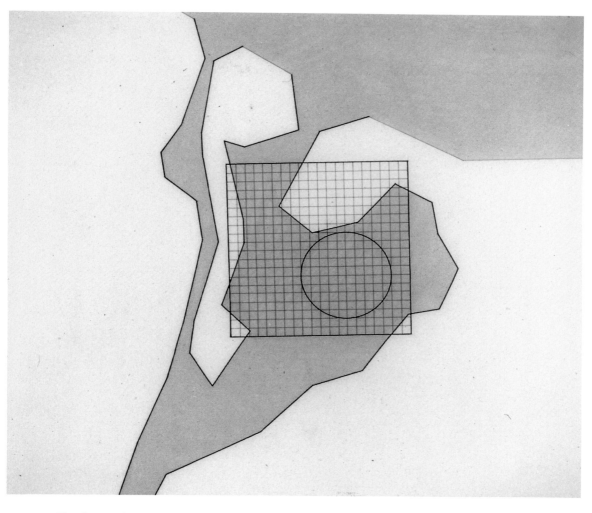

Sketches on the facing page show the formal
orthogonality and polygonality superimposed (top) and
the emergence of the third dimension. The concept's
basic guidelines — the square, the circle, and polygonal
form — are clear in the drawing above.

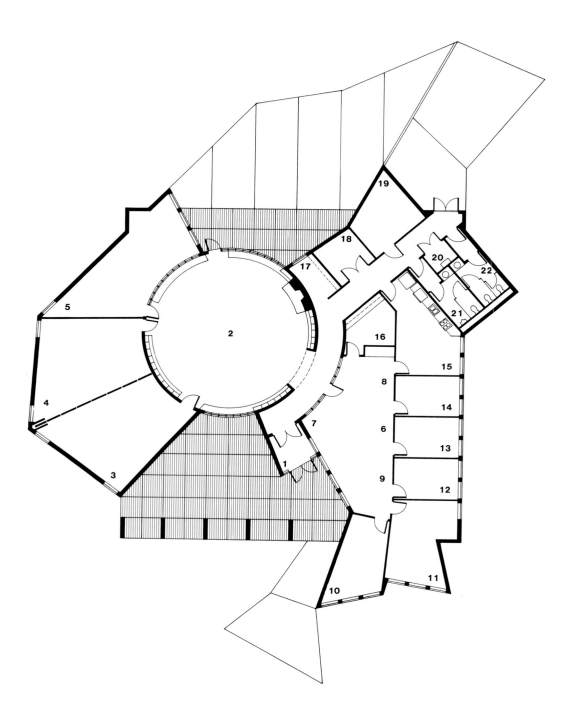

PLAN KEY

1	Vestibule
2	Honors Lounge
3	Seminar Room
4	Seminar Room
5	Library/Study Room
6	Receptionist/Secretary
7	Reception/Waiting
8	Office-Secretary
9	Administrative Secretary
10	Director's Office
11	Conference Room
12	Assistant Director's Office
13	Assistant Director's Office
14	Academic Advisor's Office
15	Kitchen/Workroom
16	Office Supply/Files
17	Coat Room
18	Storage Room
19	Mechanical/Electrical/Telecommunications
20	Janitor's Closet
21	Men's Restroom
22	Women's Restroom

SECTION KEY

1	Seminar Room
2	Honors Lounge
3	Entry
4	Office Supply/Files
5	Kitchen/Workroom

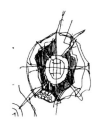

45,000 Seat Sports and Civic Stadium

Venice, Italy, 1989

(In Process)

The need to construct a new stadium for Venice presents an unprecedented challenge and opportunity. The urban fabric of Venice has been repaired, infilled and restored, but never before has it received a major civic space addition. The responsibility is enormous.

Historically, the major urban civic structures have been the Duomo, the Piazza and the Stadium. In Venice we have the first two, but the stadium is noticeably absent. It is a large urban artifact and, functionally and socially, belongs at the center of activity, in the immediate city itself. However, due to land constraints within Venice, the structure has to be taken out of the immediate city area. Thus, "if we cannot bring the stadium into Venice, we have to bring Venice to the stadium."

Since the stadium is a physical and visual part of the city, it has to express the city's architectural vocabulary. However, as an urban satellite this megaform cannot depend on surrounding vernacular. It has to be Venetian, not a universal, generic form which could be inserted into any city in the world!

The proposed image is strong and expressive. In its design, there is a strong allegiance to the Venetian vernacular with the use of water, bridges and arcades. The arcaded building form is mirrored (reflected) in the surrounding shallow reflecting pool. The analogy is extended further with the six bridges over the water leading into the spectator area.

In the year 1240, Boncompagno da Signa said about Venice:

"*. . . citta che ha pavimento il mare, per tetto il cielo e per pareti il flusso delle acque.*" [It is a city where the pavement is the sea, the roof is the sky and the walls are the flow of water.]

The new stadium has to carry the image of Venice.

Excerpted from a presentation made during a press conference in Venice, 1992.

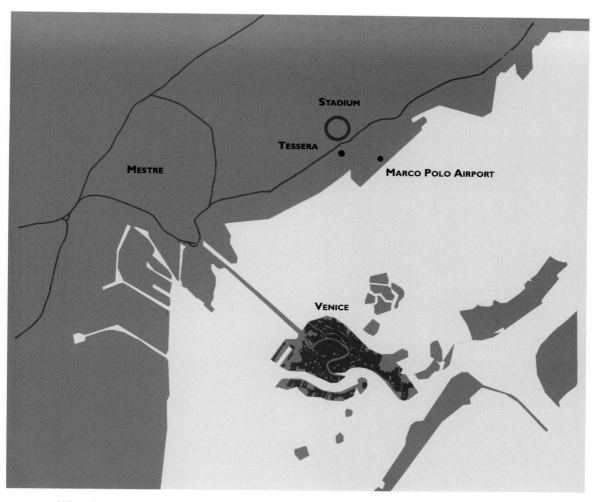

When I'm asked where in Venice the stadium will be built, I
usually answer Piazza San Marco. When the shock wears
off, I show the site near Tessera and Marco Polo airport.

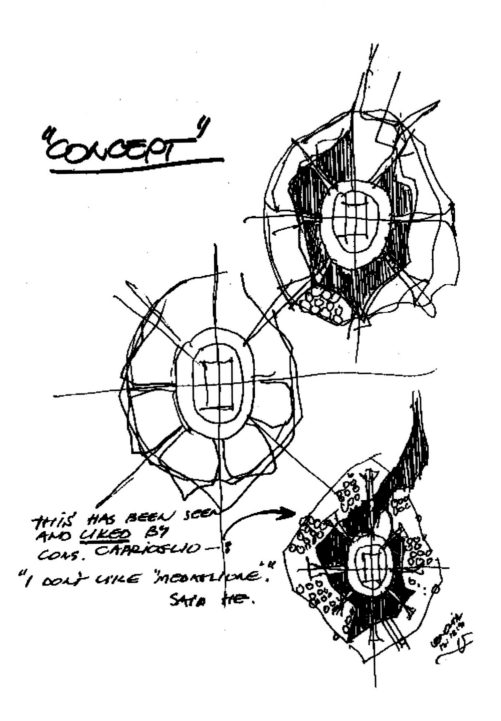

"CONCEPT"

THIS HAS BEEN SEEN
AND UKED BY
CONS. CAPRIOGLIO—

"I DON'T LIKE "MEDAGLIONE".
SAID HE.

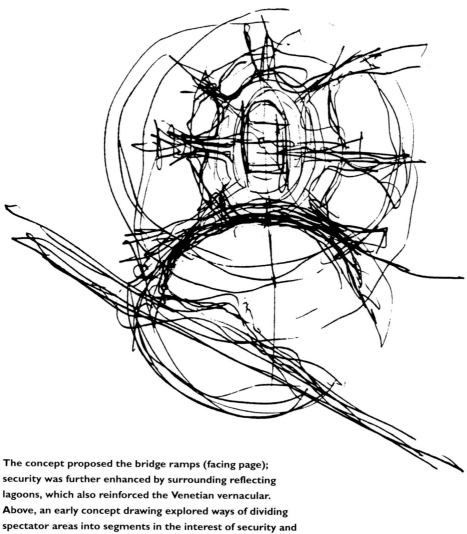

The concept proposed the bridge ramps (facing page);
security was further enhanced by surrounding reflecting
lagoons, which also reinforced the Venetian vernacular.
Above, an early concept drawing explored ways of dividing
spectator areas into segments in the interest of security and
crowd control. Circulation influenced the concept of the
bridge ramps for crowd dispersal.

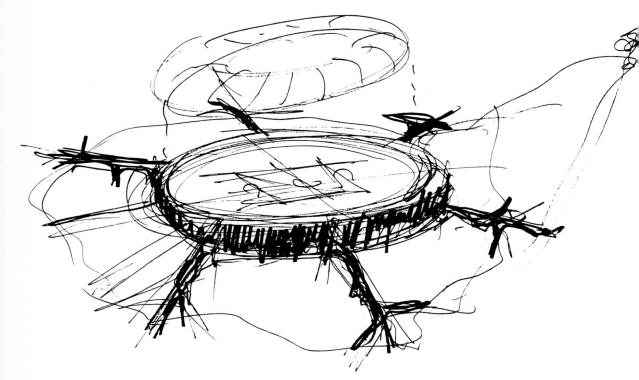

The first three-dimensional sketches visually
expressed the circulation concept and began to
crystallize the form language for the lagoon —
canal, bridge, and ramp.

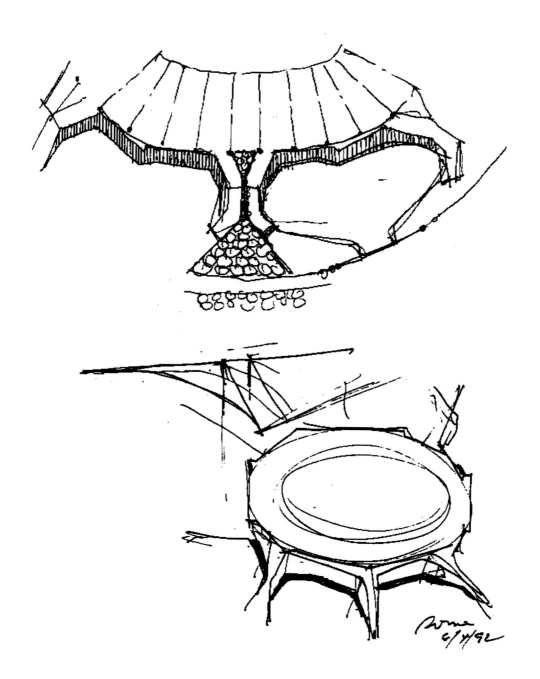

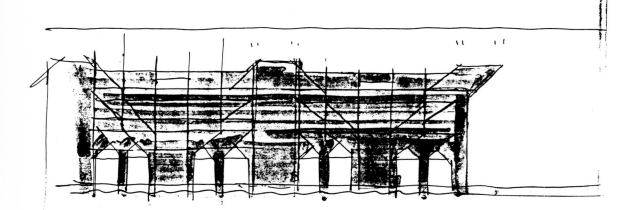

Facade studies in precast concrete technology incorporated some historic vernacular references.

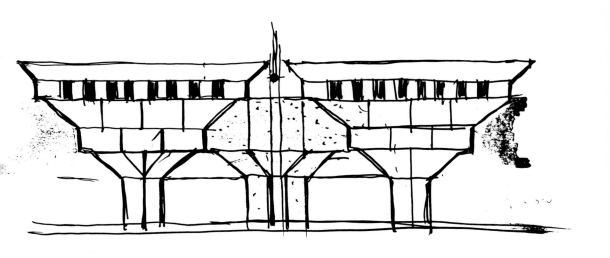

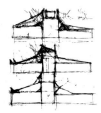

Kemper Museum of Contemporary Art and Design

Kansas City Art Institute

Kansas City, Missouri, 1991

(Under construction)

The Kemper Museum project is unique as it departs from the principles I have set and followed throughout my career. I have pledged not to attempt any conceptualization without direct contact with the user and the direct, personal opportunity to interview the clients and to write a program rather than be given one. The fact that this was an invited competition with a limited number of participants had something to do with changing my mind. We were informed that there would be only four architects participating: Steven Holl, Michael Graves, Seligson-Daw, and ourselves. Besides that, I knew Kansas City quite well and have a soft spot for it. I found a way to work with the site, and the program was rather simple. The following is a statement that followed the competition entry:

> The dynamic building form is expressive of the constant progression of modern art. It relates to context without overbearing geometry. It presents the distinct personality of the museum while using an informal vocabulary that is not related in any architectural historical style, yet it is expressionistic and accommodating.
>
> The free-flowing interior space unfolds as it progresses. It is not compartmented, but allows flexible transitions from one space to the next, from one gallery to the next and to the atrium. The weaving of nature into the building form establishes a visual dialogue with the context and a space for outdoor exhibitions.
>
> It is envisioned that architectural concrete, limestone or brick as well as glass, bronze or stainless steel may be the exterior materials. The interior palette may include wood, ceramic tiles, plaster and the appropriate covering for the gallery wall surfaces.
>
> The building represents its own and unprecedented image. I do not think of it as a style to be emulated, but a standard for design quality and responsiveness.

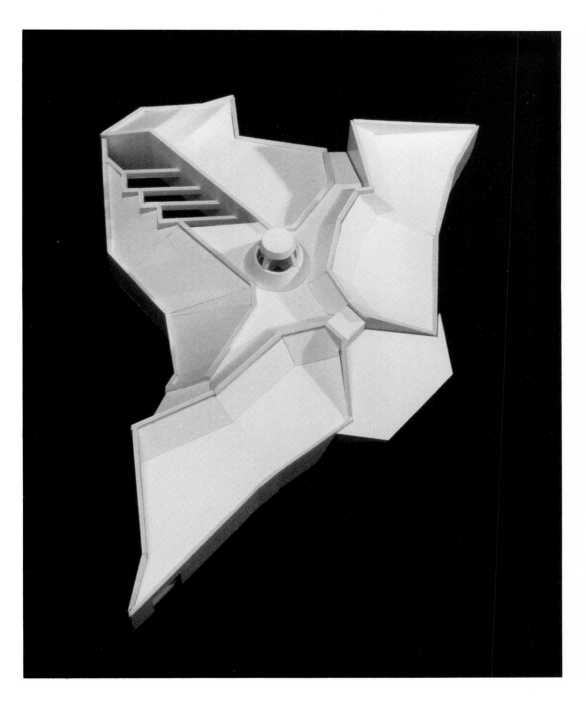

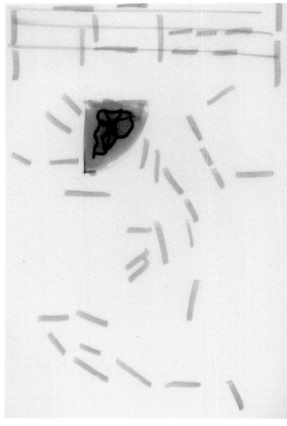

Above, an area plan with architectural vernacular analysis (left) and a site plan showing response to architectural context. This image was subsequently condensed into the preliminary conceptual form of the building. On the facing page, conceptual sketches gave the first indications of an embryonic program space.

The series of drawings shown on pages 154-55 searched for functional space relationships within the conceptual form and began to develop program space magnitudes.

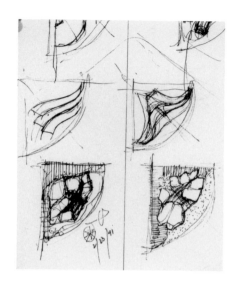

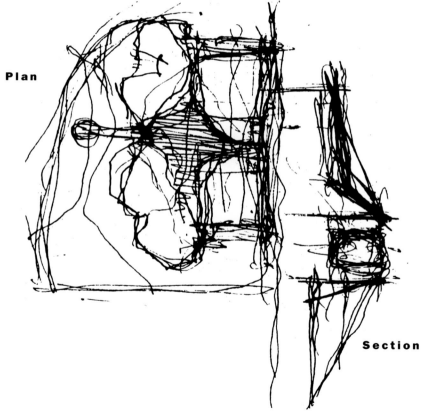

Plan

Section

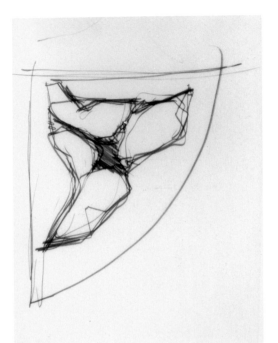

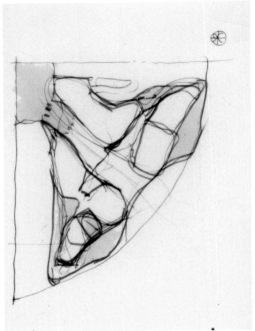

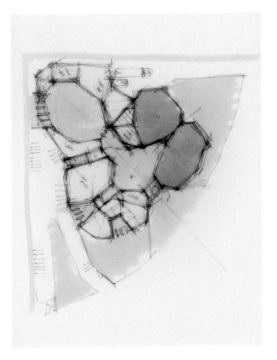

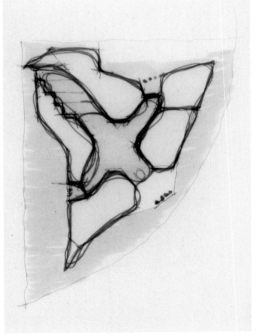

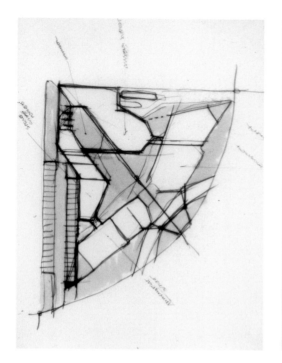

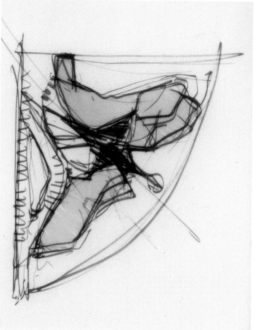

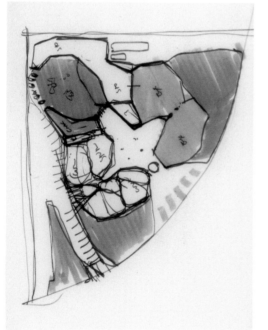

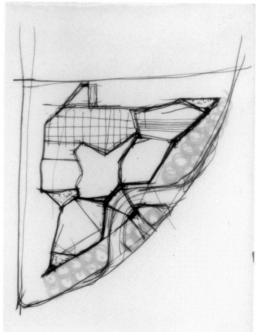

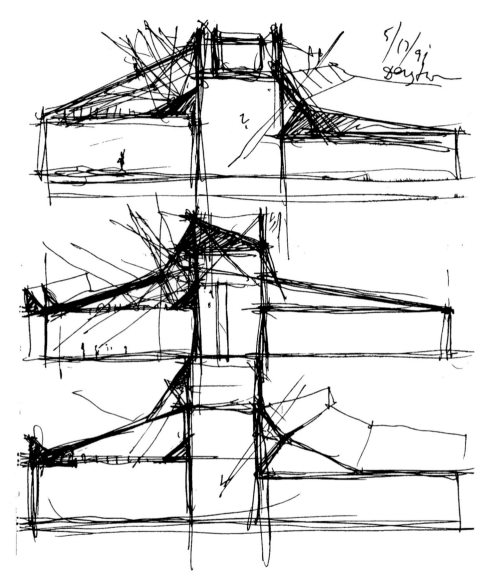

Studies in daylighting the gallery
space. The search for vertical
expression.

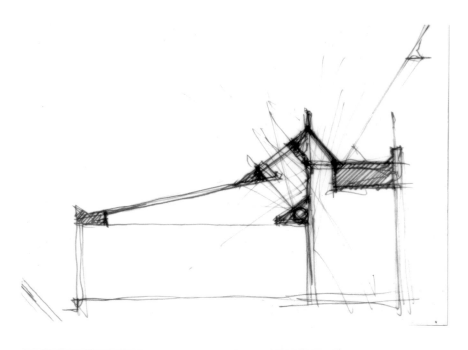

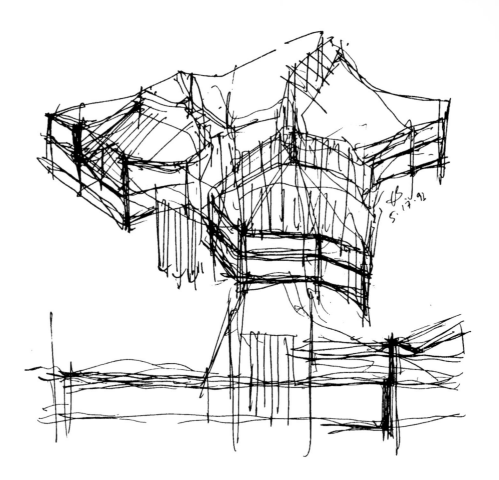

Three-dimensional form studies.

FACING PAGE: The first plan proposal with spaces sized according to program, arranged following the concept.

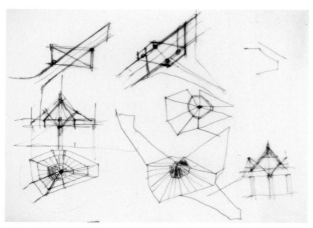

WARWICK BLVD.

45TH ST.

WALNUT ST.

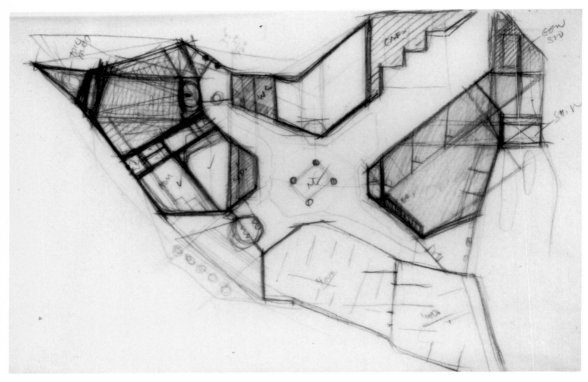

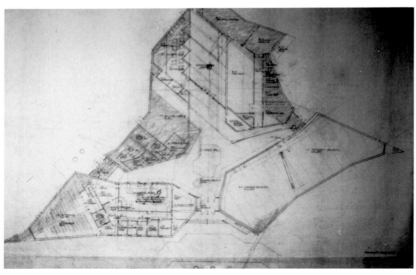

The beginning of
plan development
(top) is elaborated
in later drawings as
work sessions
proceed.

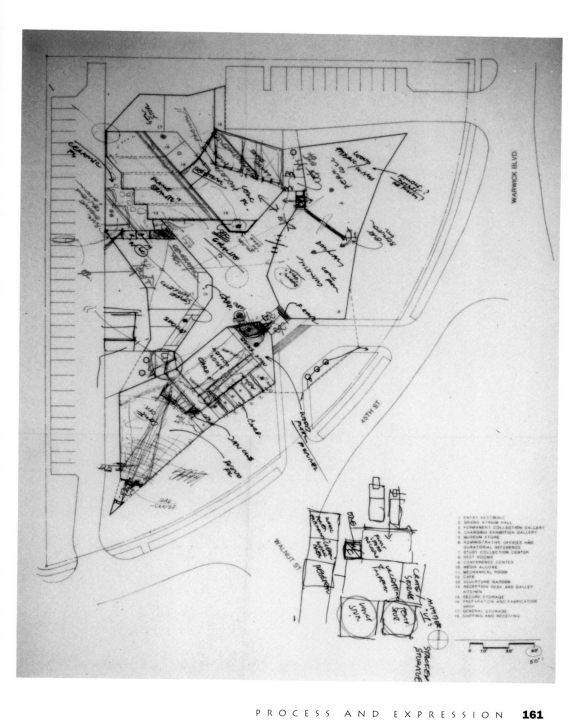

1 ENTRY VESTIBULE
2 GRAND ATRIUM HALL
3 PERMANENT COLLECTION GALLERY
4 CHANGING EXHIBITION GALLERY
5 MUSEUM STORE
6 ADMINISTRATIVE OFFICES AND
  CURATORIAL REFERENCE
7 STUDY COLLECTION CENTER
8 REST ROOMS
9 CONFERENCE CENTER
10 MEDIA ALCOVE
11 MECHANICAL ROOM
12 CAFE
13 SCULPTURE GARDEN
14 RECEPTION DESK AND GALLERY
  KITCHEN
15 SECURE STORAGE
16 PREPARATION AND FABRICATION
  SHOP
17 GENERAL STORAGE
18 SHIPPING AND RECEIVING

Keiichi Miyashita

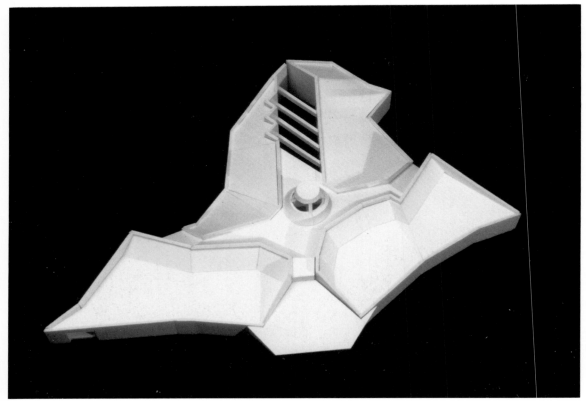

Early models of the building.

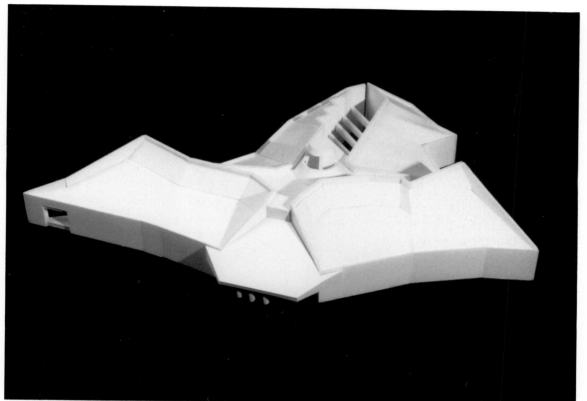

Keiichi Miyashita

AFTERWORD

Bruce Alonzo Goff served as director of the University of Oklahoma School of Architecture from 1947 to 1955. During his short but influential tenure, he designed internationally known projects such as the Bavinger House, recent recipient of the American Institute of Architects prestigious Twenty-Five Year Award. As a teacher, he helped establish the school's pedagogical commitment to nurturing creativity in design, a legacy that survives today.

To extend and reinforce that legacy, friends and former students of Bruce Goff and the College of Architecture established an endowment in 1990 to create and support the Bruce Alonzo Goff Professorship of Creative Architecture. This professorship regularly brings renowned architects and designers to the University of Oklahoma College of Architecture to work with students and mutually to explore the creative process in design.

Accounts of that exploration and the special creative perspectives of the Goff professors are documented in the Bruce Alonzo Goff Series in Creative Architecture. These volumes are intended to offer insight into the thoughts, aspirations, values, and creative processes of some major contemporary architects and designers who, through their attainment of new levels of creativity, honor the life and vitality of Bruce Goff.

Process and Expression in Architectural Form, the first book in the series, focuses on the work and creative process of Gunnar Birkerts. An iconic figure in contemporary architecture, Birkerts has invested his virtually boundless creative energies in an organic process of form-making and design. This volume offers an extraordinarily intimate and personal view into the mind and the heart of one of the twentieth century's most prolific and creative architects.

A debt of gratitude is owed the many friends and associates of the late Bruce Goff and to W. H. Raymond Yeh, former dean of the University of Oklahoma College of Architecture. Without their energy, vision, and generosity, neither the Goff professorship nor this publication series would have been possible.

Portions of the text were influenced by discussions and presentations held as part of the Bruce Goff Professorship Seminar. A word of thanks is due Professor Eleanor Weinel, seminar coordinator, and her students, all of whom contributed to the scope and depth of the discourse.

JAMES L. KUDRNA, AIA

Susan Trager-Brozes

ABOUT THE AUTHOR

1925 Born in Riga, Latvia
1945 Enters Technische Hochschule, Stuttgart, Germany
1949 Receives Diplomingeneur-Architekt degree from Technische Hochschule,
      Stuttgart, Germany; Arrives in the United States
1950 Works in the office of Perkins and Will, Chicago
1951 Joins the office of Eero Saarinen in Bloomfield Hills, Michigan
1954 Named Young Designer of the Year, Akron Institute of Art
1955 First Prize, International Furniture Competition, Cantu, Italy
1956 Joins the office of Minoru Yamasaki in Birmingham, Michigan
1959 Establishes own practice, Birkerts & Straub, Birmingham, Michigan
1961 Assistant Professor of Architecture, University of Michigan
1962 Establishes Gunnar Birkerts and Associates, Birmingham, Michigan
1963 Associate Professor of Architecture, University of Michigan
1969 Professor of Architecture, University of Michigan
1970 Elected Fellow, American Institute of Architects
1971 Gold Medal in Architecture from Tau Sigma Delta; Honorary Fellow, Latvian
      Architects Association; Fellow, Graham Foundation
1975 Gold Medal from American Institute of Architects, Detroit

1976 Architect in Residence, American Academy in Rome

1980 Gold Medal, Michigan Society of Architects

1981 Arnold W. Brunner Memorial Prize in Architecture, The American Academy and Institute of Arts and Letters

1982 First recipient of the Lawrence J. Plym Distinguished Professorship in Architecture at the University of Illinois

1984 First recipient of the Thomas S. Monaghan Architect-In-Residence Professorship in Architecture at the University of Michigan

1986 Honored for Outstanding Achievement by the Association for the Advancement of Baltic Studies

1988 Michigan Arts Award, Arts Foundation of Michigan; "Domino's 30" Award, Top 30 Architects for 1988, Domino's Pizza Inc.

1990 Distinguished Professor, The Association of Collegiate Schools of Architecture; Honorary Doctorate, Riga Technical University, Latvia; first recipient of the Bruce Alonzo Goff Professorship of Creative Architecture at the University of Oklahoma

1991 Elected Member, Latvian Academy of Sciences

1993 Visiting Professor, Lawrence Technological University, Southfield, Michigan

Additional References

Futagawa, Yukio, ed. *GA Architect 2: Gunnar Birkerts Associates, Inc.* Tokyo: A.D.A. Edita Co., Ltd., 1982.

Birkerts, Gunnar. *Buildings, Projects, and Thoughts: 1960-1985.* Ann Arbor: University of Michigan College of Architecture and Urban Planning, 1985.

Kaiser, Kay. *The Architecture of Gunnar Birkerts.* Washington, D.C.: The American Institute of Architects Press, and Florence, Italy: Centro Di, 1989.